In Search of a
New World Order

In Search of a New World Order

The Future of U.S.-European Relations

Henry Brandon, Editor

The Brookings Institution   Washington, D.C.

Copyright © 1992 by
THE BROOKINGS INSTITUTION
1775 Massachusetts Avenue, N.W., Washington, D.C. 20036

Library of Congress Cataloging-in-publication data:

In search of a new world order : the future of U.S.-European relations
/ Henry Brandon, editor.
     p. cm.
Includes bibliographical references and index.
ISBN 0-8157-1058-5 (cloth)
1. Europe—Relations—United States.   2. United States—Relations—
Europe.   3. Europe—History—1989–   4. United States—
History—1969–   5. Cold War.
D1065.U515   1992
303.48′27304—dc20   92-10578
                                                                    CIP

9 8 7 6 5 4 3 2 1

The paper used in this publication meets the minimum requirements of
the American National Standard for Information Sciences—Permanence
of Paper for Printed Library Materials, ANSI Z39.48-1984

To Muffie and Fiona

Foreword

THE COLD WAR HAS PASSED into history, and we are fortunate to contemplate a future without the threat of the Soviet Union's nuclear arsenal. This dramatic change, however welcome, presents an array of new problems that require new solutions.

Analyzing these new problems involves assessing the prospects for monetary and political union in Europe, evaluating the economic and financial influence a united Germany will have within that union, and gauging what sort of role Britain will play in this new configuration. It also means examining the future of NATO, whose function, now that the main threat from the East has faded, is being questioned and whose relationship to a European defense force is being hotly debated. An even more fundamental question is the future role of the United States in this new Europe.

As the twelve members of the European Community were preparing to meet at Maastricht in December 1991, Henry

Brandon, a Brookings guest scholar, long-time Washington correspondent for the London *Sunday Times*, and author of many volumes, proposed a book on the future of American relations with the new Europe. Because the changes are so far-reaching and fast-moving, Brandon selected eight leading personalities from five countries—Britain, France, Germany, Italy, and the United States—to give their views on the new order in the wake of that historic meeting. He is most grateful to these contributors for their cooperation in preparing these essays.

Caroline Lalire edited the manuscript, Michael Levin and Adrianne Goins checked its factual content, and Susan Woollen prepared it for typesetting. Louise Skillings and Ann Ziegler provided secretarial support. Jane Maddocks prepared the index. Because of the great timeliness of these essays, we decided to forgo the usual formal review and verification procedures established for Brookings research publications.

The views expressed in this book are those of the individual authors and should not be ascribed to the trustees, officers, or other staff members of the Brookings Institution.

April 1992   Bruce K. MacLaury
Washington, D.C.   President

Contents

Contributors

GIOVANNI AGNELLI is chairman and chief executive officer of Fiat S.A.

KURT BIEDENKOPF, a former general secretary of the Christian Democratic party and member of the German Parliament, is minister president of Saxony.

HENRY BRANDON, a former correspondent for the London *Sunday Times* and author of many books, is a guest scholar at Brookings.

JEAN FRANÇOIS-PONCET, a former French minister of foreign affairs, is a senator and an influential columnist for *Le Figaro*.

LEONHARD GLESKE has recently retired as a member of the Directorate of the Deutsche Bundesbank.

DAVID OWEN, a former foreign secretary in a Labour government, is a member of the British Parliament.

MICHEL ROCARD is a former prime minister of France and plans to run for the presidency in the next elections.

JAMES SCHLESINGER is a former U.S. secretary of defense, secretary of energy, and director of the CIA.

MICHAEL STÜRMER, an unofficial foreign policy adviser to Chancellor Helmut Kohl, is head of the "think tank" Stiftung Wissenschaft und Politik.

Henry Brandon

1

The United States
and the New Europe

A NEW WORLD ORDER is unfolding before our eyes at a breathtaking speed, and this collection of essays, written by men with a profound knowledge of the turns and tensions involved in its creation, is an attempt to assess the far-reaching impact it will have on the relationship between the United States and the new Europe and, more generally, on world stability.

The aftermath of the Cold War era has seen the sudden domino-like collapse of communism, with its dismissal as an ideological challenge and the dismantling of the Soviet Union. Western Europe is hurrying into the twenty-first century to become a new power center of its own, while Eastern Europe is in grave danger of sliding back into the nineteenth century, divided and quarreling over its ancient, petty but deep-seated nationalisms. And Germany, reunited, has become, almost inevitably, the economic middle-European powerhouse.

A fundamental question asked now on both sides of the

Atlantic is, how will this new world order affect American-European relations, world stability, and economic prosperity? History, alas, does not offer any reliable guidance to what that answer will be. The economic, political, environmental, and human rights problems the world is facing are unprecedented; not only are they of a magnitude never encountered before but they are different in kind, though some are necessarily familiar. Presidents George Bush and Boris Yeltsin have agreed to drastically reduce their nuclear arsenals; a number of other leaders have not agreed as yet. The discovery, hard-won by the United Nations in the wake of the Gulf War, of an amazingly advanced nuclear and chemical arms production capability in Iraq demonstrates how relatively easily such weapons programs can proceed, unknown to the outside world despite the contributing role of Western industries. Other countries, too, may develop, or may have already developed, nuclear capabilities or other means of mass destruction without the outside world being able to intervene.

This situation reminds me of my visit to Cuba in 1962, on the eve of what became the "Cuban missile crisis," when I, by chance, witnessed the unloading of the first medium-range Soviet missiles to be aimed against the United States. We now know that at that time a few tactical nuclear missiles had already reached Cuba. If President John F. Kennedy had not forced Nikita Khrushchev in time to withdraw all of them, including those still at sea on their way to Cuba, the action could have triggered the most dangerous confrontation of the post-1945 era. This incident remains a measure of how important it is to prevent the proliferation of nuclear missiles or of scientists capable of helping fresh countries to build them.

The price of survival under these novel circumstances will be the application of new ideas and new concepts of leadership. The North Atlantic Treaty Organization (NATO), for example, will have to adjust its mission to address future defense problems, but it will also have to adjust to the new reality that economic rather than military strength will become a major gauge of power. The United States and Western Europe will have to adapt their diplomacy—in fact, their relationship—to a new situation, one of greater equality in terms of influence and power. To explore these changes is one of the aims of this book.

The birth of a European union comprising about 340 million people is an amazing reversal of the 400-year experience of nurturing different national, economic, financial, and industrial interests. Jean Monnet, a far-sighted French businessman who had been sent to Washington by Winston Churchill to be deputy chairman of the British Supply Council, was its intellectual obstetrician. He managed to enlist support for his idea among many important Americans not only because Americans like to support causes but because he had convinced them that this new Europe would help share the American responsibilities of world leadership. As Henry Kissinger put it in his memoirs, "Monnet stressed that a united Europe would collaborate with, rather than challenge, us."[1] In those days Europeans greatly welcomed American leadership. What troubled them was not whether American power should be exercised but whether they could rely on its being exercised at moments of danger. In those days I and other European correspondents in Washington had considerable difficulty in persuading our editors and readers that they could have faith in the reliability of the American commitment. Then and even now the problem of transatlantic relations was and is to have faith in the reliability of what Europeans consider a volatile governmental system that tends to speak with many, often contradictory, voices. Admittedly, as presidents from Truman to Bush proved from time to time, there was some practical meaning in Ralph Waldo Emerson's suggestion that "in skating over thin ice our safety is in our speed."

In 1973 Secretary of State Henry Kissinger was "eager to
believe" in Monnet's ideas, as were many other Americans.[2]
"Every postwar American administration," Kissinger wrote
in his memoirs, "had supported the idea of European political
unity based on supranational federal institutions. Only a federal
Europe, it was believed, could end Europe's wars, provide an
effective counterweight to the USSR, bind Germany indissol-
ubly to the West, constitute an equal partner for the United
States, and share with us the burdens and obligations of world
leadership."[3] However, it was not long until Kissinger, as well
as some Europeans, saw a conflict between Atlantic unity and
European identity. In fact, he readily admitted that he preferred
to deal with European governments on a bilateral basis rather
than through the European institutions in Brussels. To him, at
least, it was not only a more practical way of conducting diplomacy but also one of less "skating over thin ice." But
history assumed its own, unexpected speed.

A mere two years ago the fate of the European Community
(EC) was still in doubt, yet today Europeans are imbued with
a feeling of tentative optimism because of the willingness to
submerge religious, social, and cultural differences. The drive
toward closer and closer unification is now progressing faster
than anybody might have expected or even hoped. That a new
global power is in the making is the general belief. The Community's trade, monetary, agricultural, and industrial policies
are bound to have a profound and far-reaching global effect.
Much of its power will depend on whether it will grow deeper,
or wider and shallower, as more countries hand in their membership applications. It is worth remembering Monnet's warning that only two kinds of confederations exist: those that
transform themselves into federalism, like the United States,
and those that fail.

Because so many nations are eager to join, including Sweden
and Austria, whose applications are hard to delay, the European

union, despite French resistance and the discomfort of the EC leadership in Brussels, is certain to expand faster than had been assumed earlier. Nevertheless, countries like Czechoslovakia, Poland and Hungary, however anxious they are to join the club, will have to wait. They are still too unfamiliar with the workings of democracy and free-market economics, and could get disillusioned, even rebellious. Iurii Afanas'ev, a former member of the USSR Supreme Soviet, offered a simple warning why former communist countries lack the economic basis for democracy when he said that the individual is not an independent economic entity.

But to come back to the European union, much will depend, too, on its inner strength and cohesion as it expands, because one underlying aim of the union is to enable Europe to stand up to the political, economic, and financial challenges of the United States and Japan. Another aim is to help spread liberal democracy and market economics on a global scale. Although largely supportive of European union in the past, Americans have more recently expressed doubts about how much of a united Europe the United States government would welcome and how America-friendly the new Europe will turn out to be. President Bush raised this key issue at a NATO meeting in Rome in November 1991 when he asserted, "If, my friends, your ultimate aim is to provide independently for your own defense, the time to tell us is today."[4]

For Americans it is obviously important to know how much of an American role the Europeans would want in helping them to shape answers to critical European problems. NATO, for instance, which has lost some support among Western Europeans but, ironically, has gained some from Russia and Czechoslovakia, will have to adjust its missions, especially if a European defense force comes into being. The Americans certainly would not want the Europeans to hold an American trump card to play when it suited them. Even though international security is no longer threatened by a full-scale East-West confrontation, threats to regional stability based on border disputes and national, ethnic, and religious conflicts could lead to dangerous instabilities. What should contribute to easier relations is that the Eastern bloc's surrender was not forced on it by grim human and material losses, as usually happens at the end of wars. No bitter feelings of defeat poison the atmosphere; on the contrary, the ideological victors have provided generous material help to the newly emancipated.

To come to grips with the intricate national perspectives on the future U.S. relationship with the new Europe is a formidable task. It has meant finding experts willing to reach for the imponderables of future history and, irrespective of the contradiction implied in this wording, to consider how these are likely to be influenced by current plans and outlooks for the future. Although one expert's view cannot be interpreted as representing a national outlook or that of a government, the sum of their estimates should provide some general guidance to where we are heading.

To introduce the contributors briefly, I begin with *Giovanni Agnelli*, chairman of the Fiat Group, which not only controls important enterprises in Italy, Russia, and the United States but is also one of the largest foreign investors in France. He writes about the industrial policies needed to meet the new competitive challenges to industry and about the importance of developing ways to resolve industrial disputes. He believes trade problems will assume such an importance that the GATT (General Agreement on Tariffs and Trade) organization will need further strengthening, since more and more industries are asking government help to protect their interests and thus reduce competition. He goes far in predicting that Europe will move to a federal system like the American.

Because of Germany's critical role in determining Europe's future, I asked three outstanding German personalities—experts in finance, foreign affairs, and politics—to explain how they see that role being played. *Kurt Biedenkopf* knows more about Germany than most, for not only has he been general secretary of the Conservative party (CDU), a member of Parliament, and a managing director of a leading German industrial company, but he is now minister president of Saxony, the most heavily populated and most important eastern German republic. In his current position he has been in intimate contact with the problems of German reunification. Because of the emphasis on economic issues, it is often overlooked that the democratization of former communist states also includes basic changes in the legal system. Even to make people trust the law is a major problem. So is the fact that the distribution of wealth becomes only more difficult as a society becomes richer. Biedenkopf also reminds us of the repercussions Russian and Ukrainian economic recovery will have on Western Europe and the United States. What adds to his qualifications as a judge of transatlantic relations are the years he spent as a student at Georgetown University, in Washington, D.C., where he received a master's degree in law.

Michael Stürmer writes about German foreign policy. He is so much an expert in this field that Chancellor Helmut Kohl has used him as an adviser. His main occupation, though, is that of director of a "think tank," Stiftung Wissenschaft und Politik, at Ebenhausen, near Munich. Earlier, as a professor or research fellow, he practiced at a number of universities (Harvard, Princeton, the Sorbonne, and Toronto). He is also a columnist for the *Frankfurter Allgemeine Zeitung*, considered to be very influential in Bonn.

Leonhard Gleske, a member of the Directorate of the Deutsche Bundesbank, recently retired, acts as a guide through the labyrinth of financial policies. In particular, he describes the problems Germany faces in adjusting its economic superiority to the European Community and surrendering the authority of Germany's powerful central bank, and the problems to expect when the dollar is no longer the only anchor of stability for the monetary system of the West.

David Owen, who contributes a British view, has a reputation for independent outspokenness that has characterized his whole career. Though a former foreign secretary in a Labour government, he has repeatedly been wooed, to no practical effect so far, by Conservatives. He retains a middle-of-the-road idealism that has survived the party he helped to create—the Social Democratic party—which he hoped might implement his ideas, only to prove again that in Britain to attempt such a plan is like trying to swim on a grouse moor. He remains a member of Parliament, and because of his quick intellect and political bravura, he is in unusual demand as a speaker. Owen takes a pessimistic view of European attitudes toward the United States, which, he believes, are growing "profoundly antagonistic."

Senator *Jean François-Poncet* is a former French foreign minister and a moderate Conservative. In his regular column in the well-respected newspaper *Le Figaro*, he contributes much wisdom to public thinking. He is optimistic about the future of a united Europe but expects trade problems to churn up dangerous obstacles to transatlantic cooperation.

Michel Rocard, a moderate socialist, served as prime minister of France until he was forced out of office by President François Mitterrand. He is now sharpening his knives to compete for the presidency in the next elections. He strongly believes in a European union that can look after its own safety and its economic independence without upsetting transatlantic relations.

James Schlesinger contributes a balanced American postscript to the mix of European views that is based on long experience in government, academia, and the business world. If anybody has the wherewithal to interpret imponderables, it is he, with his unusual acuity and knowledge of the great issues of our day. By training he is an economist, and as former secretary of defense he is well equipped to judge what will be necessary to protect the security of the United States in the absence of the Soviet challenge. As a one-time director of the Central Intelligence Agency he is bound to have learned a lot about the hidden capacities of governments involved in gauging world situations. Having also occupied responsible positions in the Budget Bureau and Office of Management and Budget, the Atomic Energy Commission, and the Department of Energy, Schlesinger has some concrete ideas about why the "clasping of hands" across the sea will in the future be less firm, about what sort of a role is left for NATO, and about whether the widespread fears of Europe turning into an economic "fortress" are justified. Overall, he provides some final crowning thoughts on how most of the leading issues raised in this book will affect the United States.

History, as is obvious from these pages, is hard put to catch its breath, but the hard way, as Walter Lippmann once said, is the only enduring way. From statesmen to ordinary citizens, the momentum of events always threatens to catch us unaware. It is hoped these pages will help us to advance, in Tennyson's words, "down the ringing grooves of change."

NOTES

1. Henry Kissinger, *Years of Upheaval* (Little, Brown, 1982), p. 138.
2. Ibid., p. 139.
3. Henry Kissinger, *White House Years* (Little, Brown, 1979), p. 81.
4. William Drozdiak and Ann Devroy, "Bush Challenges Europeans to Define U.S. NATO Role," *Washington Post*, November 8, 1991, p. A1.

David Owen

2

Atlantic Partnership
or Rivalry?

T HREE MAJOR TRADING BLOCS will face one another in the next century, and how they cooperate on keeping an open world trading system will affect not just international prosperity but international peace. The North American Free Trade Agreement negotiations involve the United States, Canada, and Mexico, which have more than 360 million consumers and a $6.2 trillion gross domestic product; Japan and East Asia (excluding China) have 510 million consumers and at present a $3.7 trillion GDP. These two blocs are predicted to change places in GDP ranking within twenty years. Europe—that is, the countries in the Community and the European Free Trade Association—now has 380 million consumers and a GDP of $6.5 trillion. By 2010 Europe will have a single market that includes many more countries, which gives it the potential to remain first in GDP ranking. Unlike the other two blocs, Europe has more on its agenda than just increasing economic growth; it has an ambitious political agenda.

Since the end of the Second World War, the United States has cleverly tried to bind all three blocs together, forming important Atlantic and Pacific linkages that have made cooperation and partnership stronger than competitive and protectionist instincts. In focusing on Atlantic cooperation and partnerships, I wish, without being alarmist, to raise deep and fundamental questions. The current emphasis in Europe on a purely "European Europe" diminishes the formidable contribution that the United States has made to European economic recovery and democratic stability and can continue to make, particularly with the breakup of the Soviet Union. The vision of a United States of Europe is one that fails to see the strength at various times of the contribution of the individual member states of the European Community. Europe is starting to breed attitudes that are profoundly antagonistic to the continuation, let alone the development, of the Atlantic partnership.

THE SHAPE OF THE EMERGING EUROPEAN UNION

The shape and character of the emerging European union, to be achieved by the start of the twenty-first century, is still a mystery. It will rightly be far more than a mere free trade area. Yet whether it will emerge as a single state with a merged political identity is uncertain. Relying on history, one can peer ahead and guess at the likely influence of individuals, but no one can be sure of what sort of union will develop.

The British Position

The view from the United Kingdom is to stress the need to retain a Europe of nation-states within the movement toward greater unity, whereas political leaders on the Continent appear ready to accept a single European state. There are some echoes of the British viewpoint in public opinion in Germany and France, and this discrepancy between what the public and what politicians think is bound to produce change. The question is, will the politicians shift public opinion or will public opinion change the attitude of politicians? In Britain the debate for too long concentrated on whether we should join the movement toward European unity at all; it continued from 1962, when we first seriously contemplated entering what was then called the Common Market, until as late as 1989, when the Labour party finally reconciled itself to membership as a permanent feature of life in Britain.

Britain has signed many treaties in its long history, but none has had anything approaching the same significance as that incorporated within the 1972 treaty that brought Great Britain into the Community. At the time of signing, Parliament and the British people were assured that no commitment inherent in the treaty would force them to abandon the United Kingdom as an independent sovereign state. Without such categoric assurances, undoubtedly Britain would never have joined. Few, however, were blind to the reality that we were joining an evolving Community. In 1974 Lord Denning, one of our great judges, said, "When we come to matters with a European element, the Treaty is like an incoming tide. It flows into the estuaries and up the rivers. It cannot be held back."[1] Even now, twenty years after we became a member for good or ill, the European Community tide is still eroding our shoreline and penetrating our countryside.

All Community member states are committed to "an ever closer union" by the Treaty of Rome, but that begs the question of what sort of union. A bookmaker taking bets on the future of Europe would set the longest odds against the member states keeping the sinews of their nationhood. The reason is that many continental European politicians draw their inspiration from the founding fathers of the Community, such as Jean Monnet,

Robert Schuman, and Paul-Henri Spaak, and have never questioned that the course on which the Community embarked in 1956 would lead inexorably to a United States of Europe. Nevertheless, the Maastricht Treaty, signed in February 1992, may provide the focus for a change in the constitutional direction of the Community. To succeed, such a change will have to arise from a public reassertion of pride in nationhood in either Germany or France. This is not to advocate a rebirth of rabid nationalism but to advocate quiet patriotism.

The German Position

All the leading German politicians over the last two decades— Chancellor Helmut Kohl for the Christian Democrats, Chancellors Willy Brandt and Helmut Schmidt for the Social Democrats, and Foreign Minister Hans-Dietrich Genscher for the Liberals—have been committed to a Germany that will pool all aspects of its sovereignty within the Community. This unabashed enthusiasm and persistent advocacy for a single European state is still coming from all the leading politicians in what appears to be a self-confident united Germany. Germany is the richest and most populated of the Community states and is particularly well placed to provide the political dynamic for the Community. Soon Germany will be geographically at the hub of an enlarged Community. Austria, Poland, Hungary, and Czechoslovakia, as well as Sweden, Finland, and Norway, are all likely to join the Community by the end of the century.

Thereafter in the early part of the twenty-first century, Community expansion will probably include Slovenia (perhaps linked with Austria), Estonia, Latvia, Lithuania, and maybe Croatia. Possible other members will be Switzerland, Serbia, Bulgaria, Rumania, and Albania. One may see Ukraine and Belarus pressing for entry. A Community of more than thirty nations is now widely accepted as being inevitable by the year

2010, and the German language will be the second language for most of these northern and eastern Europeans. Although there is still some hesitation in defining the outer limits of the Community, many admit there would be real problems in absorbing two countries that are both Asian and European: the Russian federation and Turkey. A strict definition of Europe would not allow them to become full members even though Turkey is already an associate member. Yet associate membership might well be extended to the Russian federation and even to Israel.

A crucial determinant of the future will be German public opinion. In an assessment made at the end of 1991, the Rand Corporation found that for the first time a majority of Germans opposed further integration of Germany into the European Community. Also, a majority was against any U.S. forces or nuclear weapons continuing on German territory. Such attitudes to the U.S. military presence in Germany are not new. The opposition hardened through the 1980s and is likely to have been reinforced by the addition of East Germany. There is, however, no such easy explanation for why a majority has turned against a single currency; perhaps Germans now realize it means the abandonment of the deutsche mark. Nor are there obvious reasons why a majority now opposes any further political union. Opinions may change, but it is as if, their own unity having been achieved, most Germans feel more eager to take pride, as they have every right to do, in their country's freedom and independence.

The British, as distinct from the French, tend to think this change in Germany is a perfectly natural development and neither to resent it nor to fear it. For some years British public opinion has seemed confident that postwar Germany is a firmly rooted democratic state. Prime Minister Margaret Thatcher, in her opposition to reunification, tried to fan public fear of a Fourth Reich, but the attempt met with virtually no public response. Even with Germany taking a more independent stance over such foreign policy matters as the recognition of Croatia, and with the British government disagreeing with the German government's position, British public opinion has not reacted. Diversity, as viewed from Britain, is part of a democratic European Community. Uniformity reflects either a bureaucratic, unadventurous lowest-common-denominator Community or an authoritarian Community, neither of which has any appeal.

The French Position

In France, where the Gaullist tradition of anti-American sentiment in foreign policy continues, there has up to now been little protest from the Center or the Right as President François Mitterrand has subtly moved the French position toward advocacy of ever greater European integration. Mitterrand has looked ready to accommodate and even at times champion a union for the Community that will become a single state. French politicians' enthusiasm for ever greater integration is justified to their voters by the supposed need to lock Germany into the Community so as to prevent a resurgence of German nationalism. Germanophobia is still surprisingly strong in France despite the recent history of quite remarkable Franco-German accord. Built first between Chancellor Konrad Adenauer and President Charles de Gaulle, this rapport has continued ever since across party political divisions and is well exemplified by the close relationship between Mitterrand and Kohl. The formal French position, as presented in the December 1991 Maastricht negotiations, still leaves open the possibility that the Community will remain a union of nations and will not develop into a single United States of Europe. French diplomacy is, however, deeply ambivalent on this issue.

Until Germany forced the recognition of Croatia in January

1992, the Quai d'Orsay's view was that French interests would always predominate, and the government was content to accept majority voting even in foreign policy. This self-assured viewpoint, widespread throughout the French civil service, stems from France having astutely infiltrated all the key decision-making positions in the Commission in Brussels. But recently Commission attempts at fundamental reform of the Common Agricultural Policy and the conduct of Competition Policy challenging "French first" attitudes have suggested that France is not getting its own way as frequently as it used to. At present these minor inconveniences are tolerated by Paris, and Brussels' actions have not as yet stirred French politicians into action. Only if the French viewpoint in the Community continues to erode, and if that becomes obvious to public opinion, will existing politicians be likely to challenge the current direction of France within the European Community.

At the next French presidential election in 1995, President Mitterrand will not be standing; however, the likely candidate from the French Socialist party, Michel Rocard or Jacques Delors, is far more committed than Mitterrand to a United States of Europe, as is former president Valéry Giscard d'Estaing, leader of the Liberal UDF. The former prime minister Jacques Chirac, leader of the Gaullist RPR, while against too much political integration, is ambivalent because French business sees benefits from integration. It is the far-right-wing politician Jean-Marie Le Pen who now speaks most effectively against complete integration. No longer representing a mere protest vote, he aims to become "Monsieur 20 percent" and to force his way into a partnership of the Right. To Le Pen, those who support a United States of Europe are *fédérastes*, and *mass-trich*, or mass cheating, is what happened at Maastricht.

The British interest is in a new and younger voice emerging from either the Center-Right or Center-Left in France, to match the caution that Prime Minister John Major has astutely shown about inexorable movement toward the federalist vision of a single European state. Few in Britain want to see France weakening in its fundamental support for the European Community, and fortunately the conservative RPR has as little enthusiasm for that as did the Conservative party for Thatcher's hostile attitude to the Community toward the end of her reign. The younger generation in Britain, as in France, accepts that membership in the Community is both desirable and irrevocable. Yet what could emerge from the new generation of French politicians, perhaps more likely from within the RPR, is a quiet, confident, and respectable assertion of French nationhood and a determination that it should never be totally submerged within a European state. It is hard to understand why such a combination of commitment to the Community and commitment to retaining the nation-state has not yet found its political voice in France. Such a position could help kill off any further advance by Le Pen and might inhibit the far Right elsewhere in Europe. It is worrying that the extreme Right is beginning to develop its appeal in a number of other European countries, particularly in Austria.

THE MAASTRICHT TREATY

In Britain the Maastricht Treaty has been greeted with a mixture of boredom over its detail and perhaps premature relief that the federalist dream has been repulsed. Most of the media reporting has focused on the international politics of the Conservative party. Britain's postponement of a decision on joining a single currency and its refusal to sign the social charter were seen as the price for Conservative unity. Far too little attention was given to the underlying structure of the treaty.

The significance of this treaty is that instead of the expected

tree-like treaty, with all branches stemming from the Commission, a different, temple-like treaty emerged, with independent
pillars on foreign, defense, and monetary policy. Only one
pillar, that relating to the single market, stems solely from the
Commission. The single-market pillar is thought by almost
everyone to be very desirable, and it will be the powerhouse
for Europe's economic growth. Most Britons accept an open
trading system, and more are criticizing the current agricultural
subsidies for Community exports; there is no serious pressure
for European protectionism. But all that could change in a
climate in which a European Europe turns its back on the
Atlantic partnership.

The approach to Maastricht was a difficult negotiating process. Britain, Italy, Germany, and the Netherlands fortunately
were in agreement on defense and the need for keeping NATO.
Britain and France were in partial agreement on foreign policy,
wanting to remain independent permanent members of the U.N.
Security Council and ready to keep the Commission out of
foreign policy. Germany, Britain, and the Netherlands wanted
any European Central Bank to be totally independent. These
combinations ensured that it was possible for intergovernmental machinery to be accepted only as the vehicle for a common
foreign and security policy. Also, independence for the Central
Bank was an absolute requirement for making progress toward
a single currency. The word *common*, as distinct from *single*,
in Community parlance means that an individual member state
has the freedom in the last analysis to act independently, and
countries are not bound by majority voting procedures.

Foreign Policy

It is symptomatic of the growing German ambivalence to
integration that despite their previous advocacy of a single
foreign policy and majority voting, Germans were loud in pro-

claiming an independent line when faced by what they thought were their vital interests in Croatia. It was in my view an unwise decision, but a strength that the Maastricht Treaty wisely allowed for taking such a line. A common foreign and defense policy is to be pursued "by establishing systematic cooperation between Member States in the conduct of policy . . . implementing . . . joint action in the areas in which the Member States have important interests in common." Maastricht also states that "common foreign and security policy shall include all questions related to the security of the Union, including the eventual framing of a common defence policy, which might in time lead to a common defence."

Instead of creating a Defense Community, as nearly happened in 1954, it was decided at Maastricht that the Western European Union should "elaborate and implement decisions and actions of the Union which have defence implications." The WEU already has a working relationship with NATO, and this was not only the least threatening way of establishing a European pillar within NATO but an overdue use of an appropriate vehicle. But France clearly will go on pressing for a European defense that excludes America. Only when confronted by the need for U.S. Air Force heavy-lift capability for the quick deployment of forces are the French generals able to limit their politicians' rhetoric. That the French wish for a binary relationship with North America rather than a partnership that bridges the Atlantic is more worrying now than when they broke with NATO's integrated command structure, because it is a more widely shared view among other European countries.

Economic Policy

A European Central Bank, by being made totally independent of the Commission and of national and European parliaments, ensured another independent pillar, something that was adamantly demanded by the German Bundesbank. Whether a single currency emerges by 1997 for the key Community countries, however, depends on economic developments in the United States and Japan as well as Europe. Britain's reservation at Maastricht arises from the political magnitude of the decision and not just as a way of ditching Mrs. Thatcher's opposition. Yet despite British doubts, if Germany still wants a single currency badly enough after the 1994 election, then that will probably happen. If at that time the British Parliament believes that an independent foreign policy has still been preserved, it may well, though reluctantly, agree to become an initial member of the single currency grouping. The reasons will be connected with Britain's overriding need to maintain London as Europe's principal financial center against competition from Frankfurt, where the Central Bank will almost certainly be located. But if public opposition to losing the deutsche mark grows in Germany, then the much maligned hard European currency unit could even reemerge as a more acceptable currency for Europeans traveling and doing business across national boundaries. The hard ECU would be a common European currency existing alongside national currencies. However, so strong is the momentum now toward a single currency, it is a good bet that national currencies will disappear.

A single European currency once in position will mean a massive erosion of economic sovereignty and will be a significant step toward a single European state. Margaret Thatcher believes it makes a single state inevitable. I am not sure. Since the Community is developing as a unique international body, it may prove possible to have a single currency while never going beyond a common foreign and defense policy. Yet for such a constitutional arrangement to be trusted and relied on, it needs to be part of a constitutional settlement. Those who fear that a single currency leads irrevocably to a single foreign

and single defense policy, and therefore to a single state, need
to know that the escalator toward a single state has been de-
liberately slowed down.

CONFLICTING ATTITUDES WITHIN
THE COMMUNITY

Since Maastricht the stance of those Europeans committed to
a United States of Europe has become obvious. It is to pretend
that Maastricht was but part of the continuity of treaty making
that started with the European Coal and Steel Community,
which preceded the creation of a Common Market. Such Europeans scoff at any attempt to interpret the compromise of
Maastricht as a crossroad for the Community's development,
with a new road opening up. Their strategy, devised as the
temple-treaty was being constructed against their will, is to
collapse its independent pillars as soon as possible into one
pillar based on the Commission and a European Parliament.

In a letter to the London *Times* of January 29, 1992, Sir
Roy Denman, a distinguished former British civil servant who
went on to work for the Commission in Brussels and then
represented the Community in Washington, wrote that the peoples of Europe ''are moving inexorably (with Britain as always
shuffling ten years behind) to a Union where national governments will be reduced to the role of local authorities.'' He did
not even give national parliaments the status of California or
Massachusetts in relation to Washington. It was noticeable that
the German Länder were more concerned about any erosion
of their powers at Maastricht than the German Bundestag. In
Britain, not surprisingly, the Scottish Nationalists campaign for
''independence in Europe'' and are among the most passionate
supporters of a United States of Europe. It is logical that within
a single state, separatist movements in other parts of Europe

see similar opportunities. Belgium might not remain a single entity in a United States of Europe, and even Spain might find its territorial integrity threatened.

It is a strange paradox that at a time when the USSR has fragmented into many separate independent nations and when the Yugoslavia federation is doing the same, the majority of European states seem only too eager to move to a union based on merging into a single United States of Europe. As more American people watch the House of Commons daily on satellite television, with a mixture of amazement at the behavior of MPs and some admiration at the way our prime minister is personally held to account, they are better placed to understand why many in Britain will stoutly resist our Parliament becoming a mere local authority in a United States of Europe. Yet it may sometimes appear that such resistance is reactionary, dated, and nostalgic. To many Americans it seems a natural development for a United States of Europe to emerge over the next few years. But American politicians should ask whether such a development is in the interests of the United States, just as more politicians in Europe are asking themselves whether a United States of Europe is in the interests not only of their own country but of the sustainable goal of European unity.

The single European market, which starts in 1993, is already almost totally governed by Community directives having the power of law in the member states. The single market will be policed by the Commission and the European Court, and will be democratically accountable primarily to the European Parliament. It is already a very powerful unified voice within the GATT. To create a single market and process the myriad of directives, it was felt necessary even by the Thatcher government in 1986 to accept the fact that related decisions would be taken by a qualified majority. The complexity of the directives, unlike foreign and defense policy decisions, was felt to require a formalized voting procedure. That could be just as

necessary when the Community starts to integrate the economies of the former communist countries within its single market. Majority voting is weighted so that in the Community of
Twelve, a British national position can be overridden by 54
votes. Britain, Germany, France, and Italy each carry 10 votes;
Spain has 8 votes; Belgium, Greece, the Netherlands, and Por-
tugal 5; Ireland and Denmark 3; and Luxembourg 2.

Many British parliamentarians like myself, long-standing
believers in the European Community, have been able to accept
such a formula for weighted majority voting as being a necessary pooling of sovereignty to achieve a desirable economic
objective. Yet for overriding political reasons, we do not accept
such a procedure to achieve a single European defense policy
or single foreign policy, for we know that if Europe was allied
to a single currency, it would become to all intents and purposes
a single state. It would be a state of many languages; three at
least—English, French, and German—would be working languages. Such a state would also have difficulty in achieving a
single legal system. More important, it would be a nation in
which the cultural and ethnic divisions would be as great as
in any past empires that have subsequently dissolved. Such a
European state, even if it emerged democratically, would, I
believe, eventually dissolve in disharmony.

CONCLUSION

One advantage of the debate prior to Maastricht was that majority voting was acknowledged to be a mechanism designed
only for supranational government. It is noteworthy that NATO
functioned throughout the Cold War as the most effective international organization that has ever been devised, without
using formal votes or having any institutional mechanism for
majority voting. NATO's strength lay in the patient, persistent

search for unanimity and on the good sense of the member states in not pushing their opposition to its ultimate point of dissent when they found themselves in a clear minority of the member states.

In the WEU Treaty there is similarly no provision for majority voting; democratic accountability is to an assembly composed of members of the national parliaments. Provided the WEU Treaty language remains the same as now, and even if it formally becomes one of the European Community treaties to apply to all new members, it contains nothing that challenges the essentials of nationhood or the continued partnership of Europe and the United States in NATO. The WEU is designed as a vehicle for international cooperation. Strengthening the WEU is not an escalator toward a United States of Europe or a vehicle for the destruction of NATO; it is a rational way of reflecting the reality of European defense in the 1990s. A European Defense Community linked to the Commission and the European Parliament with majority voting would, by contrast, be far more threatening to NATO. France needs to be dissuaded from pushing for such a single defense policy over the next decade.

European countries will have to take a larger share of the burden from the United States within NATO than hitherto, and to do so there is merit in a coherent European view sometimes being coordinated by the WEU in advance of NATO meetings. But it is in Europe's interests for the United States to keep some forces assigned to NATO based in Europe. Such U.S. forces will be far smaller than before, which should give no cause for concern. If U.S. forces are totally withdrawn, however, it will not be long before America sees its own security starting only at its shoreline. Of course, the breakup of the Soviet Union means that change in NATO is desirable, but that applies to the United States as much as to Europe. Perhaps now that the nuclear deterrent needs less megatonage, it will be possible to have a European as supreme allied commander as well as secretary general of NATO. Britain and France will, it is hoped, move closer on nuclear policy and perhaps make a formal assignation of their nuclear submarine deterrent to the WEU. But the deliberate driving of all U.S. forces back across the Atlantic is dangerous in defense terms and disastrous politically.

Just as it is both an American and a European interest to keep NATO, so I believe it is a joint interest to keep European foreign policy as ultimately a responsibility of national governments. Under the Maastricht Treaty, a unanimous decision is required before any voting procedures involving a qualified majority can be introduced. This means that neither France nor Britain, as permanent members of the Security Council of the United Nations, can have its hands tied. Both are free to co-operate with the other three permanent members. It also means that a British prime minister need not be inhibited in making decisions on foreign policy that he or she feels to be in the national interest. The importance to the United States of this appears sometimes to be forgotten. Those Americans who often rather naively endorse a United States of Europe as if it were a logical development analogous to that of the creation of the United States of America would be well advised to ask what the attitudes and policies of a United States of Europe would be. Would they be as compatible with America as those of the existing system of European nation-states? There have been and will again be moments when U.S. national interests and British national interests coincide and when France or Germany, or both, have not been prepared to support U.S. policy. That has often been true in regard to Israel and to the handling of terrorism.

There exists a European reluctance to authorize the use of force as a tool of international policy which the British government does not always accept. For example, Britain sent a task force to retake the Falkland Islands, allowed U.S. F-111 aircraft to fly from bases in Britain to Libya, and sent British land forces to Saudi Arabia to help the United States buttress sanctions and then attack Iraqi forces in Kuwait and in Iraq itself. I do not want to imply, however, that Britain alone has had any monopoly on courage or wisdom in foreign policy; France over the years has also been ready to deploy forces in difficult circumstances worldwide. What is important to stress is that some of the great independent nations of Europe that have had colonial responsibilities and maintain interests outside Europe—France, Germany, the Netherlands, and Spain— need to be free to show the sinews of their nationhood when their vital interests are at stake. Allowing this degree of diversity in foreign policy will not weaken, but rather strengthen, Europe's collective response.

What I envisage is a unique European union that respects nationhood and seeks not a European Europe but a Europe that remains part of the Atlantic partnership. That would ensure a European union of member states ready to play a constructive role in the world as part of a trilateral grouping of free-trading democratic nations.

NOTE

1. *Bulmer* v. *Bollinger*, 2 A11 ER (1974).

Michel Rocard

3

Toward a Redefinition of Transatlantic Relations

THE COLD WAR ERA, dominated by devastating, ideological adventures, ended with the failure of a coup in Moscow and a breach in the Berlin Wall. As this page in our history closes, some are afraid we have reverted to the last century, and they predict a new world catastrophe. The temptation is indeed strong to view the Cold War as a lost paradise of peace (but surely our memories are not that short) and to see no other solution but to reinforce the institutions and policies it gave birth to.

It is true that Europe is in danger of falling prey to tensions which have spared it until today. It would indeed be irresponsible to imagine a totally cloudless future: democracy is slow in taking root. The temptation of authoritarianism remains strong here and there, and for a long time to come nationalism will be the exaggerated expression of newfound liberty.

But let us not succumb to the easy temptation of pessimism, even if it is the expression of a dismay that is quite understandable given the magnitude of the recent changes. In December 1991, at Maastricht, the Europeans showed their dynamism, their ability to rise to new challenges, and they paved the way toward an exacting, yet exciting, common future.

To promote a "new world order," President George Bush has called for new actors to appear on the international scene and for new forms of dialogue between them—in short, for the redefinition of the machinery of international cooperation. In recent decades transatlantic relations have been more than just the expression of an unfailing solidarity among allies; they have been the mainstay of the international order born of the Cold War. With the end of the Cold War it is only natural that transatlantic relations should undergo some changes, that the solidarity between the United States and the states of Europe should enter a new phase. It is doubtless too early to propose a new global organization for the planet; let us be humble enough to recognize our doubts and our uncertainties, but let our ambition come to terms with some simple principles on which to base the solidarities of tomorrow.

TRANSATLANTIC RELATIONS AND THE END OF THE COLD WAR

The Cold War set the European continent apart, which protected it from new conflicts. It was first destroyed, then divided, and finally over-armed. Europe punctuated world events with crises and upheavals. But Europe has also shown that dialogue and cooperation between fierce rivals are always possible: the Conference on Security and Cooperation in Europe, a pioneer in the 1970s, laid down principles that many others have since adopted, and the revolutions of 1989 revealed the immense political vitality of the old world. And the European summit in Maastricht opened up unprecedented political prospects.

An unusual era for Europe, beset with strife, suffering, and worry, is passing in a spirit of reconciliation. An era heavy with constraints—the constraints of the balance of terror—has come to an end.

After the Second World War Western Europe rebuilt its prosperity, thanks largely to the aid it received from the United States under the Marshall Plan. But it was unable alone to assume its own security in the face of the crushing superiority of Soviet military power. Its contribution was far from negligible, and was in any case always courageous. Three features characterized the Cold War period and shaped transatlantic relations.

The first was bipolarity: the organization of the world built around the ideological rivalry between the two great victors of 1945. It obliged every nation, as a last resort, to take sides. The political alliances that stood face to face were therefore, of necessity, the decisive actors on the international political scene. This arrangement did not exclude internal differences of opinion, as long as what really mattered, namely East-West competition, was not undermined. France is no doubt the country that made the best use of this leeway to make its own political choices, particularly with regard to the Third World.

The preeminence of the political alliances was reinforced by the second characteristic feature of this period: nuclear weapons. The two superpowers were the first to master nuclear technology and subsequently to build up vast arsenals of nuclear weapons. When fear of the apocalypse became the basis on which world peace was built, East and West embarked on an endless quest for more sophisticated nuclear weaponry and strategies; and nobody could ever be sure that the other side was sufficiently afraid. Peace reposed on this fragile but undeniable balance; it was America's strategic nuclear forces that prevented the Soviet Union from attempting a military adventure in Europe.

The idea of this linkage gave rise to some serious differences of interpretation, leading France to withdraw from the NATO military command, or caused pacifist movements to protest the deployment of Euromissiles, the purpose of which, one should not forget, was to counterbalance the SS-20s deployed by the USSR. But nobody doubted that the very principle of transatlantic linkage was the strongest guarantee Europe could have facing the Soviet Union. Personally, I have always been close to the United States and considered its solidarity as Europe's greatest protection in the aftermath of the Second World War.

The third feature characteristic of this period was the creation of a permanent institution designed to respond to the dual threat, political and military, from the Soviet Union that hung over Europe. The debate over whether NATO has a political foundation or is a strictly military organization is futile. The Cold War was a system in which politics and the military were inextricably bound.

These different factors created a situation that was not always comfortable for Europeans, for the corollary of this peace was immobility. The arms race moved in a relentless, infernal spiral to which there seemed to be no end. "No war" meant peace, but it also meant division.

Europe's recovery from the aftermath of war called for a readjustment. Its renewed prosperity led the United States to ask for a better distribution of the burden. Who would dispute that when the risks were shared, the costs and responsibilities should also be shared?

The disintegration of the communist bloc accelerated Europe's awareness of its own specific political identity and sped it along the road to unity. That is why, as early as April 1990, France and Germany called upon their partners to pursue not only economic and monetary union but also political union, with responsibilities in the fields of foreign policy and security. This is the goal toward which the member states of the European Community decided at Maastricht to work together.

Only the recognition of the political identity of these states, which are currently twelve in number, can bring about a new style of transatlantic relations capable of facing up to the international issues we will have to deal with in the coming years. It will mean relinquishing some of our traditional references and rising together to meet new challenges.

NEW STAKES AND NEW ACTORS ON THE INTERNATIONAL SCENE

The democratization of central and eastern Europe and the subsequent disintegration of the Soviet Union have profoundly altered the face of Europe. It rapidly became evident that the best guarantees in the face of the risks of instability lay in speeding up the process of unification on which the twelve states had already embarked. Far from being an exclusive club reserved for the winners of the Cold War in Europe, and determined, like the aristocrats of the ancient régime, to hold on to their privileges rather than sharing them, the economic and political union of the Twelve is the central core of a process affecting the whole continent. It is no longer a question of whether the new European democracies will be members of the European Community—they are so in line with their calling. The question is when, how, in what form, and for what purpose. Meanwhile, progress on the building of a united Europe will help the Community to contribute more effectively to the stability of Europe as a whole.

The lesson we must learn from the experience of recent years is that confrontation is not an unavoidable fate. The events of late 1991 and early 1992, however, have also demonstrated that avoiding confrontation requires a determined effort. Those who claim that people are prisoners of their history are defeatists who insult the memory of those who fought and suffered to overthrow communism. The last forty-five years cannot be considered a historical parenthesis in a Europe condemned by its very nature to tear itself apart. At least, a politician like myself cannot condone such reasoning; to believe in politics is also to believe in the ability of men and women, states and societies to look beyond their past history to build the history of the future.

In this respect Maastricht represents a great step forward. The building of the European Community, which the Cold War helped to encourage, reflected the determination of the people of Europe not to have to fight one another in order to be stronger, more prosperous, and more stable. We have achieved this objective, and the disappearance of the threat of communism has given this objective a new dimension: that of bringing peace and prosperity to the whole continent now that the Cold War is over.

In 1945 the United States dreamed of a world without ideological, economic, or cultural barriers. The sovietization of Eastern Europe soon eclipsed that fine ideal. Today the prospect of a more cooperative world has been reborn, but to prevent it from being overrun again by the din of battle, we must make sure that the organizations and procedures we establish to encourage integration and cooperation are strong enough to face up to the multitude of issues facing us in an increasingly complex and interdependent world.

It is my belief that the regional organizations have a major part to play in the integration process. Their strength lies in their ability to respond both to the particular interests of societies and states and to the planetary challenges that they confront. In other words, the two pitfalls we must avoid are selfishness and the lack of a proper identity.

Thus far in the building of Europe we have managed to avoid these pitfalls. Thanks to the path traced out at the summit meeting in Maastricht, we will continue to avoid them in the new European context. The Twelve have set themselves a target and endowed themselves with the procedures and machinery to achieve it. Economic and monetary union will come first, based on thirty years' experience of successful cooperation. Political union will take longer to succeed, for it affects the heart and sovereignty of nation-states. There will be differences of opinion, but let us not be too harsh: a lot of ground has been covered since Maastricht! The process of European union is now irreversible, and I rejoice in this.

The strength of European union lies in the fact that it proposes a specific and coherent political, economic, and social development model we might call a "social-democrat" model, one in which most European states mirror themselves today. It combines respect for the rules of the market economy with reinforced social legislation and the acceptance of a rule of law as the basis for relations between individuals and the state. These three principles together form the basis of the European model. The idea, for example, that central and eastern Europe can develop simply by adopting the purest form of economic liberalism is an illusion; it is understandable but dangerous. The market alone cannot provide social organization. Many are the crisis-ridden states that have added to the chaos in their societies by attempting to apply the laws of the market economy without any social counterbalance.

By giving societies a new say in the running of their affairs, and putting political concerns before strategic considerations, the democratization of central and eastern Europe has helped to redirect our attention toward social issues (the environment, town planning, migration, and so on). We must now adopt decisionmaking structures in keeping with the scale of these problems, which are no longer confined to individual countries.

For some time, constant reference to the rule of law has promoted the idea that certain principles must be respected by all, that they transcend the competence of national governments alone. The renewed interest in the United Nations is a reflection of this idea, and it is not unreasonable to maintain that in certain areas, such as the environment, drug trafficking, and the monitoring of human migration movements, the spirit of cooperation has triumphed over the spirit of competition.

The problems of security must be approached in a similar spirit. The military threat from the Soviet Union has given way to risks of a more diffuse kind that threaten not so much the interests of any particular state as the stability of whole regions or of the international community as a whole. Whereas the former security system was a collective one, based on the principle that an attack on one state was an attack on all, the new system might be qualified as a community security system, insofar as the main risks a state can run are those that threaten to destabilize its environment. In such a context as this, the security policies of the future will increasingly involve collective choices (no single state, for example, could interfere in the crisis in Yugoslavia) that will be impossible to plan in advance.

This changing pattern in our joint security must lead to a corresponding adjustment in transatlantic relations.

TOWARD A NEW TRANSATLANTIC PARTNERSHIP?

Transatlantic misunderstandings have arisen from time to time in the years since World War II, and the last two years have also produced their share. Yet there is widespread conviction that we have entered a different phase in transatlantic relations. The appeal launched in Berlin in June 1990 by James Baker in favor of a new Atlanticism was the first sign; George Bush followed that up with his idea of a new world order. These views were echoed in Europe by the acceleration of the machinery of European unity and the active participation of the European countries, including France, in defining a new strat-

egy for NATO and initiating a dialogue between NATO and
the countries of Eastern Europe. Today misunderstandings can
be avoided through a more evenly balanced form of partnership, both in security matters and in economic and trade
relations.

Security Matters

In the field of security, fear is particularly acute that the very
symbol of transatlantic relations, NATO itself, might be in
jeopardy. For a long time, it is true, misunderstanding marred
relations between France, anxious to preserve its policy of
independence, and the United States, whose main concern was
to maintain the cohesion of the alliance. I am one of those
people who consider that this opposition was often very dam-
aging: in those days cooperation on security matters could take
place only in the context of NATO, and I have always been
firmly convinced that security is an area for international cooperation, and regretted that Europe was not yet able to take
charge of this grand project.

Today, however, that is no longer true. NATO is undeniably
a solid reference point in a world in complete turmoil. Its
know-how, its experience must be preserved, and I for one
would be in favor of France intensifying its cooperation with
NATO. But there is more to it than that. Who can fail to see
that under the combined pressure of the disintegration of the
communist bloc and the new international stakes that are
emerging, transatlantic relations lose their world-embracing
dimension to become one piece among others in the machinery
of planetary stability?

Strangely enough, the concern over the future of NATO has
led to two largely contradictory conclusions. Some say that the
end of the communist bloc does not necessarily eliminate all
military threats from Eastern Europe, and they cast Russia in

the former role of the Soviet Union, arguing that in the face of the prevailing instability nothing should be changed. Others think emphasis should be placed on the nonmilitary role of NATO, in the name of the fundamentally political character of the organization; in this case, NATO's future would lie in its transformation into a political association with ill-defined objectives.

In my opinion, these two approaches are equally wrong and equally dangerous—for the very legitimacy of NATO. Why waste time and energy in attempting to redefine the exact nature of NATO's future role? One of the so-called new objectives of the alliance strikes me as being particularly pernicious: only NATO, the argument goes, is capable of keeping watch on Germany and avoiding its remilitarization. What strange logic is this that wants Germany to show greater commitment in times of world crisis, while at the same time worries about its remilitarization? Only the citizens of Germany are in a position to judge whether the time has come for Germany to devote more of its resources to defense; Germany's allies can only wish that its resources will be used for the collective interest. Whatever hesitancy there may be in German foreign policy will disappear only when the political context becomes clearer.

It is an awkward debate, indeed, because it cannot be reduced to stark contrasts. The question of whether NATO or the political union should take charge of the security of Europe is largely inadequate. If I have raised the question, however, it is because I know how important it is to Americans, and how many misunderstandings there have been with the French on the subject. I am deeply convinced, however, that the institutional quarrels are too dogmatic, and therefore futile and prejudicial to the real debate. If we wish to progress politically, therefore, let us put an end to this petty quarreling. What counts today is that Americans and Europeans should make up their minds how they can best work together in the interests of security. And before all else this means establishing exactly what those interests are. There are several remarks I should like to make in this connection.

1. The question of how to allocate the missions between the different defense organizations is a secondary consideration today. A distribution of responsibilities by geographic zones, leaving Europeans every latitude to act outside Europe while letting NATO be in charge of security in Europe, strikes me as being very unrealistic. Not only has the conflict in Yugoslavia demonstrated the limitations of this type of reasoning, but who can seriously expect Europeans not to be directly concerned by what happens in their own territory?

The Euro-Atlantic debate certainly seems at times to take on a surrealistic tone. And yet the question is simple enough: can Europeans be confronted on their own territory with crises that do not concern the United States? For some people the very idea was a blow to transatlantic solidarity, the risk of seeing the USSR intervene in a European crisis making the prospect of a strictly European policy unthinkable. But even before the demise of the USSR, the conflict in Yugoslavia changed all that. Rightly or wrongly, the United States decided that its interests and its idea of international stability were not at stake in this crisis, and it let the European Community act. This is the type of crisis Europeans may have to suffer on their own soil in the years to come, and it is for this reason that Europe must have the military means to support its policy, so that it is ready to act as and when required. Diplomatic mediation alone is clearly not enough.

2. In addition, the bipolar confrontation that has thus far set Europe apart from the rest of the world will soon be receding. The geographic criterion will count less than the nature of the crises to be faced. By diminishing its presence in Europe and withdrawing its tactical nuclear weapons, the United States is acknowledging the fact that with the disappearance of the threat

of Soviet aggression, the specificity of Europe is beginning to fade. Indeed, the recent war in the Gulf proved that it is possible to react quickly when the right infrastructures are pre-positioned. That was true in Saudi Arabia; and it is also, of course, true in Europe. But if it is no longer the deployment of tactical nuclear weapons and the stationing of troops that guarantee the American commitment, other mechanisms must do so.

On this point, my answer is quite clear: only the manifest determination and ability of Europeans to defend themselves can permit new transatlantic relations to take shape. Nobody can be defended against his will. I have long been in favor of a European defense system. Today I rejoice that this idea has met with a broad consensus among my fellow Europeans, who decided in Maastricht to make the Western European Union the instrument of this policy.

Europeans have decided to go ahead with political union—and this is indeed a matter for Europeans to decide—and po-litical union will inevitably extend to foreign policy and security. What meaning would political union have if it were unable to provide for its own security? It would be no more than reinforced cooperation between governments. The Franco-German initiative to set up a European army corps is in the direct line of the political union process. It would be the very symbol of European defense: what could be more eloquent than a common European army? As we all know, that is just the first stage in a long, drawn-out construction process. One should not fall into the trap, therefore, of criticizing Europeans because they are not yet able to achieve their goal, as if in so doing one hoped to prevent them from achieving it.

But there are other good reasons for Europe to have its own security policy and the means to implement it. In the days of the Cold War, the United States prevented conflicts outside Europe from degenerating by negotiating directly with the So-

viet Union. This is no longer possible. And who can say that
a militarily stronger Europe would not have been a more effective ally in the Gulf War?

The main threat to security for the future is the proliferation
of weapons capable of mass destruction, particularly nuclear
weapons. Whether they lie in Europe, in the former Soviet
Republics, or elsewhere, they are a source of concern for Americans and Europeans alike. If we wish to prevent certain states
from launching attacks on their neighbors under cover of a
nuclear threat designed above all to deter any Western intervention, Europeans and Americans must work together to define the lines of a common policy. More than a direct attack
on ourselves, what we must guard against is a proliferation of
aggressive policies that might well jeopardize international stability; any action the West might wish to take would then be
subject to nuclear blackmail. The nuclear weapons that guaranteed peace in Europe, thanks to the strategy of deterrence,
now threaten to become the instruments of new local hegemo-
nies. This new twist in events is particularly unacceptable to
a French person sensitive to the idea of dissuasion of the strong
by the weak. Only a resolute policy on the part of the West
can prevent would-be potentates from embarking on such
adventures.

3. Finally, the role of nuclear arms and of deterrence must
be redefined. As the cornerstone of the bipolar system, subject
to increasing refinements to render the U.S. commitment in
Europe credible, nuclear deterrence could return to its initial
function: ensuring peace not through the threat of nuclear war,
but through the political inacceptability of the threat of a nuclear holocaust. The time has perhaps come at last to reconcile
strategic realism and political morality.

These remarks leave a number of questions unanswered, but
the reasoning behind them is clear: the new international context calls for a redefinition of security policy. Only thus will

we achieve the more cooperative approach to the management
of international affairs to which we aspire.

Economic and Trade Relations

In economic and trade relations misunderstandings can also
easily arise. On the one hand, Americans (and indeed the Japanese) are inclined to wonder whether Europe after 1993 will
be a fortress or not; on the other hand, Europeans do not like
to see GATT negotiations leading to constraints they find hard
to accept, particularly in agriculture or certain industrial sectors,
without any concessions in exchange in such important areas
for them as financial services. To oversimplify somewhat, one
might say that the United States is afraid that European union
will spark off a wave of regionalism that will threaten the spirit
and the achievements of the GATT, while Europe fears that
globalism will favor one particular region at this stage, namely
the United States, more than the other members of the GATT.

This contrast—globalism versus regionalism—soon leads to
misunderstandings. And yet the facts are plain to see:

—It can scarcely be denied that for several decades the logic
of the GATT was in harmony with a development of international trade in excess of growth, the former no doubt helping
to boost the later.

—The European Community is henceforth the largest group
of free markets anywhere in the world; and the links to be
established between the EC and EFTA (European Free Trade
Association) members will make it even larger. This huge
group of nineteen countries is generally very open to trade
with other countries; the Community, for example, has adopted
rules particularly favorable to the developing countries. Furthermore, those central and eastern European countries that
have initiated their economic reform processes will gradually
strengthen their ties with Western Europe and the rest of the

world; Poland, Hungary, and Czechoslovakia are indeed already members of the GATT.

—The same facts apply to investment as to trade. Transfrontier investments underwent rapid growth in the 1980s, particularly transatlantic investments, in both directions. Like the United States, Europe welcomes outside investment, even if the poor reputation of certain countries (including France) in this respect, which is unjustified or no longer justified, lingers on. It is certainly easier, for example, to purchase a firm in France or the United Kingdom than in Germany or Switzerland.

So why worry? First, because the facts show that three major regional entities are emerging in the world economy: North America, strengthened as a whole by the recent legal bonds between the United States, Canada, and Mexico; Europe; and East Asia. International trade between these three regions has grown more slowly than trade within each region. The figures deserve closer examination to determine exactly what types of goods are exchanged and how reliable the figures are. But these trade differences certainly seem to be the general pattern.

Second, because each region, for different reasons, views the other two with a certain apprehension. Japan is concerned about the threat of restrictions on the expansion of its sales and investments in the rest of the industrialized world. The United States, because it really believes in free trade (even if it sometimes turns a blind eye to its own restrictive practices), considers that Europeans do not always play the game. And Europe, while it will be a major industrial power, wishes to keep the modernization of its agriculture under control, and it does not see why it should make further concessions without fair compensation in areas such as banking and services.

My approach to these questions is pragmatic; we must steer clear of generalizations and negotiate. We have solid ground on which to build: there is hardly any other time in history when great nations or groups of nations have enjoyed economic

relations so free and so lasting as those that exist between
North America and Europe.

Experience has demonstrated that when real issues are debated, agreements can be reached. I believe one of the reasons
that the Uruguay Round fell behind schedule is that we all
took too long to lay the real issues on the table—perhaps
because a certain form of dogmatic enforcement of the rules
of free trade was bound to create a situation in which Europeans
had reason to fear they could not accept them in the absence
of significant country concessions.

So I am not pessimistic about the future. There is no doubt
that we are heading toward three increasingly integrated regional entities. But this does not mean that the barriers between
these regions will not be lowered further.

The reintegration of the countries of central and eastern
Europe, the Baltic states, and what used to be the Soviet Union
into the mainstream of international trade will raise some specific problems. The concern to help these countries through
trade and with public funds will meet with a fear of dumping
all the more acute because economic growth in Western Europe
is currently very slow. It is unlikely, however, that these problems will compromise the general trends I have outlined.

This is the context in which the project of monetary union
must be analyzed. It will complete the move toward a fully
integrated market. But above all, the single currency will help
Europe to overcome the problems caused by fluctuations in
the exchange rate of the U.S. dollar; the economic agents will
come to use the dollar as a reference in their contracts and as
a reserve currency.

Conclusion

Both in economic terms and in terms of security, the building
of Europe will lead not to new tensions between Europeans

but rather to an easing of existing tensions. In agreeing on the major orientations of their future, Europeans will be in a position to contribute to the birth of a new, more balanced transatlantic partnership guaranteeing a new solidarity. And on this condition Europeans and Americans will be ready to rise together to the challenge of their common future.

Jean François-Poncet

4

Toward a Directorate of Continents

F OR MORE THAN FOUR DECADES the West stood united in the face of the communist challenge. In spite of many disagreements and crises, the United States and Europe continued to maintain close ties—ties that played a decisive role in the triumph of democracy in Europe, the end of the Cold War, and the collapse of the Soviet empire.

The alliance did not merely block the USSR's expansionist aspirations and attempts at military intimidation. By reconciling Europe's and the United States' often divergent mind-sets, the alliance made it possible to conduct a firm policy based on deterrence and a willingness to negotiate.

Basic common sense dictates continuing on a path that has yielded such good results, especially since the challenges of the postcommunist era will no doubt be more complex and formidable than those of the Cold War. Cooperation between the United States and Europe will be even more needed in tomorrow's uncertain and unstable world than in the brutal but

simple and stable bipolar universe of yesterday. This conviction
is shared on both sides of the Atlantic. No one wishes to cast
into doubt the common destiny that has been forged in all
fields—military, economic, and political—in the course of the
last fifty years.

But good intentions and a strong will are not enough. Transatlantic relations must rest upon the firm basis provided by an
in-depth analysis of the two continents' respective situations
and long-term interests. However, superficial, easily changed
views are more commonly encountered than lasting and dis-
passionate judgments. Proof of this is provided by the successive conflicting certainties of the very recent past. In the space
of a few years, opinions on the European Community have run
the full gamut. Those who held it to be suffering from Eu-
rosclerosis at the beginning of the 1980s termed it a protectionist fortress in mid-decade, before its mediocre performance
in the Gulf War and the Yugoslav crisis led them to decry its
divisions and powerlessness, predicting that it would soon fall
into the clutches of reunified Germany. Throughout the same
period, equally incorrect stereotypes have been applied to the
United States, ranging from exemplary economic dynamism at
the beginning of the Reagan years to irremediable decline in
mid-decade to sole mastery of the planet after the collapse of
the USSR.

The first task is thus to put relations between the United
States and Europe beyond the reach of gratuitous speculation
and intellectual fashion and protect them from false prophets,
sensationalist journalists, and politicians running out of clichés.
Rather, the deep and ongoing currents that shape these relations
must be identified, as well as the policies to which they give
rise.

Even if a policy, once chosen, cannot exist in a vacuum
from which are excluded the very realities to which it is meant
to apply, it must not be forgotten that the goal of policy is

often to counterbalance the prevailing trends of a given time. The post–World War II period is a case in point. Europe appeared destined for communist domination. The USSR, encamped on the Elbe, controlled powerful and often subversive Communist parties that, it was feared, might come to power in Greece, in Italy, and even in France. The wind of history seemed, as Mao Zedong put it, to be blowing from East to West. It was to block this apparently prevailing trend that the United States and its European allies pooled their wills and means.

Does a sense of history or major trend exist in relations between the United States and Europe today? If so, what policy should we adopt? What obstacles might such a policy encounter? What means would have to be put into play for it to prevail? These are some of the questions on which the future of transatlantic relations will depend.

DIFFERENCES WITHIN THE ATLANTIC ALLIANCE

Ministers' speeches are reassuring. They exalt the need for and the virtues of the alliance. But a cool analysis of reality yields less encouraging conclusions, revealing that relations between the United States and Europe are already subjected to centrifugal forces today and will be even more so tomorrow.

The most important of these forces concerns security. Confronted by the Soviet menace, defense has been the binding force of the alliance since World War II. But it seems clear that, given the disintegration of the USSR, security, as it has been defined since 1945, will no longer be the West's main concern. Still, peace is obviously far from guaranteed, and it would be illusory to believe that economic factors alone will henceforth dominate the scene, as the Yugoslav crisis, the potential civil war developing in the Caucasus, and the internal tensions stemming from the breakup of the USSR suffice to show.

It is, however, unlikely that the United States will intervene in the interethnic conflicts that threaten the Balkans and the former USSR and that might tomorrow lead to confrontations between certain Eastern European countries. Who can still believe that public opinion will accept the shedding of American blood in the upheavals of another era, none of which directly affect the United States' vital interests?

This is the source of the conundrum currently paralyzing NATO. On the one hand, Americans and Europeans unanimously wish to preserve a structure which has been proved to work and whose essential role for Europe and the new international order they affirm in chorus. On the other hand, the alliance appears unsuited to intervene in the civil war–like conflicts that threaten Europe. Signs are that even if the alliance is still the guarantor of last resort for peace in Europe and the nuclear night watchman of a continent confronted by the danger of proliferation inherent in the breakup of the USSR, it will not be able nor will it wish to appoint itself policeman in the interethnic disorders casting their shadow over the eastern part of the European continent.

In other words, different arrangements will have to be made to guarantee Europe's day-to-day security. The United States' participation in such mechanisms will, at best, be at arm's length. Conclusion: Europe's and the United States' concerns, decisions, and actions in the field of security will tend not to be contradictory but to develop in separate spheres and to implement independent means—in short, no longer to represent, as they did yesterday, the tough, workaday fabric of transatlantic solidarity. At the same time, political and geographic priorities will also tend to diverge on either side of the Atlantic.

On political priorities, most American commentators emphasize to their European counterparts that the United States, freed from its preoccupation with communism, will devote its energy to licking its domestic wounds: the school and banking systems, the budget deficit, infrastructure, inner cities, drugs, crime, AIDS, and so forth. Long neglected, these problems will take a heavy toll on human and financial resources. Why should the United States give massive assistance to the former USSR when it has so many poor people at home?

Geographic priorities will evolve along the same lines. The Cold War made Europe the United States' number-one concern for fifty years. The disappearance of the Soviet threat has radically altered that situation. The United States will henceforth take just as great, if not greater, interest in other parts of the world that are closer to home, like Latin America, or bigger players on the American economic scene, like Japan and Southeast Asia.

Europe, for its part, will be obliged to turn its sights eastward. Europe will use all possible means to avoid turning the transition from communism to a market economy and democracy into a social and political catastrophe. Europe will attempt to contain the emergence of new nationalisms and minority revolts. Heroic efforts will be made to prevent the massive migration that insecurity, unemployment, and famine might fuel. At the same time, however, Europe will have to look toward the South, where the rise of Islamic fundamentalism is a challenge all the more serious in that on its own territory live several million Moslems sensitive to currents emanating from their countries of origin.

Neither the United States nor Europe will turn its back on the other. They will, however, tend to devote themselves to their own priorities and leave their partners to do the same. One exception to this every-man-for-himself policy is the Middle East. Oil on the one hand and the Arab-Israeli conflict on the other are of as direct concern to the United States as to Europe and will oblige them to cooperate closely.

One might fear that in this context of relative distance-taking, divergences of viewpoint and conflicts of interest that have long existed could take on dimensions unknown in a period when the Soviet menace imposed absolute solidarity on one and all. This is the real danger that stalks relations between the United States and Europe.

Of all these potential conflicts, the most dangerous would appear to be trade related. This conflict has heightened within the GATT, and the negotiators' clumsiness, together with Japan's dexterity, makes the final GATT round resemble nothing less than a duel between Atlantic partners on the subject of agriculture.

The stakes being played for are, nonetheless, rather low: agricultural products accounted for only 12 percent of world trade in 1990, as against 20 percent in 1970. Moreover, the real subject of this dispute—primary commodities, basically grain and protein crops—is still more modest, accounting for only 3-4 percent of world trade. Faults lie on both sides. Agricultural support systems differ, but the amounts concerned are equivalent. The European Community makes greater total payments to farmers than the U.S. administration ($97.5 billion compared with $67.2 billion in 1989). However, when these figures are divided by the number of persons concerned, per capita aid is shown to be $20,000 per farmer in the United States and $8,000 per farmer in Europe. A draw, more or less.

Under such conditions—low stakes and faults on both sides—it should be possible to reach agreement, all the more since the United States now has a hefty surplus—about $14 billion in 1991—in its trade with Europe, which, unlike its trade with Japan, has developed very favorably. But this does not take into account passions, lobbies, and elections. Failure is possible. Some say it is likely. The economic and political consequences of failure would be catastrophic for three reasons: because world trade is the engine of economic growth, and failure in the GATT would jeopardize long-awaited recovery; because failure would in all likelihood lead to a chain reaction of reprisals and ultimately to continental protectionism as harmful to world prosperity at the century's end as national protectionism was in the 1930s; and, finally, because transatlantic guerilla warfare on trade would poison the political climate to a dangerous extent, accelerate the emergent uncoupling of Europe and the United States, and compromise EC member countries' image in the United States. The Community, though, is the new reality upon which the future of transatlantic relations will have to be built. Hence it is of paramount importance, should the spring 1992 Uruguay Round not yield the positive conclusion that all parties are hoping for, that there be, rather than a flat statement of failure, a simple adjournment of negotiations, the resumption of which should immediately be planned for after the U.S. presidential elections. In the intervening time, parties would pledge to refrain from initiatives likely to sour international trade relations.

THE NEED FOR A NEW ALLIANCE

Left to themselves, relations between the United States and Europe may well be subjected to mounting tensions that, if not mastered, would dangerously weaken the West as it confronts the formidable challenges that lie ahead.

There is awareness of this danger on both sides of the Atlantic. President George Bush and Secretary of State James Baker have, on a variety of occasions, and in particular during the last NATO summits, expressed their wish to adapt the alliance to the new demands of the postcommunist era. But the proposed reorganizational measures, whether they concern institutional balance or structure of the armed forces, do not get to the bottom of things and fail to take sufficient account of the scope of the changes that have taken place or will occur in the future.

The time has come to go further. A new alliance must be devised. New because it must no longer link the United States to separate European countries as is the case today, but rather to the twelve countries of the Community as a whole, before going on to ally the entire North American continent to a European union broadened to include northern and central Europe. New, too, because it should move toward a fair distribution of responsibilities and burdens, a fairness which is all the more logical in that economic factors will play an increasing role, as will Europe in the world at large. New, finally, because of the concerns the alliance ought to address which should no longer be limited to defense but instead extend to all challenges that require collective responses from the West.

John F. Kennedy had already envisaged a two-pillar Atlantic architecture. Henry Kissinger did the same. For many reasons, this concept never came into being. But the situation arising from the collapse of the Soviet Union requires that it be developed today.

The obstacles should not be underestimated, nor should fundamental issues be avoided, especially in the United States. One might in particular wonder if it is still in the United States' interest to favor European integration and if European union and Atlantic cohesion are still complementary.

Opinions expressed on these subjects in the United States were uniformly positive forty years ago, when the first steps toward European integration were being taken. This is no longer true today. Many feel that a unified Europe would be an ornery, difficult partner, inclined to cast doubt on the United States' leading role in the world without itself assuming the share of responsibility and burdens that it should. Conflicts, they feel, would multiply. The GATT, they say, gives an unpleasant foretaste of this, and NATO would be the first to pay the price.

To these fears must be added a technical remark concerning
the way the European Community makes its decisions. It is
rare for the Community's member states to agree among themselves at the outset. Joint positions are arrived at only after
lengthy and laborious discussion. And when the process is
over, it is very difficult for them to take their partners' views
into account. They suffer from a congenital rigidity that injects
uncertainty into compromise and threatens the smooth course
of transatlantic negotiations. Hence the United States' reluctance to let Europeans define common positions among themselves within the Atlantic alliance, which would tend to present
Washington with a fait accompli.

The reasons cited by those alarmed to see the birth of a
European bloc are thus not without cause. However, the argu-
ments of those who advise Americans to support the European
integration process, to use it as a base and to make it a part
of their own policy, are more solid and convincing. These
reasons may be summed up in two propositions: (1) without
union, there will be no stability in the Old World; (2) without
an integrated Community, the United States will not find in
Europe the partner it will need to fulfill the global responsibilities that have fallen to its part.

Lurking instability in Europe today also threatens the United
States, even if the danger is less perceptible than was that of
communist expansionism yesterday. However, the causes of
this instability run deep; economic transition is slow and ran-
dom, with sacrifices imposed on entire populations; there is
the fragility of young democracies exposed to criticism and
escalating demagoguery; nationalisms are colliding; minorities
are rebelling; the USSR has disintegrated; and so forth. The
Community constitutes the only pole of stability to set against
these tensions. EC member countries and institutions were the
source of about 80 percent of the economic and financial assistance that was committed to Eastern Europe and the USSR
before April 1992. Their markets will be the first to receive

Eastern European products. The Community's institutions are the ones Czechoslovakia, Poland, Hungary, and many other countries dream of joining. Neither NATO nor the Conference on Security and Cooperation in Europe is in a position to meet these expectations. Of course, the programs implemented by the Community and its members to assist Eastern Europe seem infinitely less effective than the Marshall Plan was in an earlier day. But the situations are not comparable. Western Europe had been physically destroyed, but was ready to go back to work, on condition that the material means to do so be provided. The implosion in Eastern Europe today is not merely material; it is social, moral, and human. Today Eastern European economies are paralyzed less by the scarcity of aid than by the lack of structures to put aid to use.

Europe is the United States' irreplaceable partner in dealing with the problems arising from Eastern Europe and the former USSR and in the global responsibilities the United States is called upon to bear in the postcommunist world.

As the sole superpower, the United States will not be able to ignore any of the tensions or conflicts that may threaten the world's security, health, prosperity, or environment. Turning its back on the rest of the world will be impossible, and refusing to accept responsibility impractical. But the reluctance of a public opinion faced with painful and recurrent domestic problems will make intervention difficult and often impossible. The United States will need partners by its side that are ready to share responsibilities and burdens. The Gulf War was a case in point. The United States did not need anyone's military assistance to defeat Saddam Hussein. But would the United States have acted alone, without the political backing of a large coalition and the massive financial contributions made by Germany, Japan, and a dozen other countries? The conclusion seems doubtful. And tomorrow, still more will be needed. The United States will need full partners, capable of sharing not only material consequences but also political and moral responsibility for decisions to be made and action to be taken.

Burden sharing, which the United States has, justifiably, been requesting from Europe for so long, will become an unavoidable necessity in tomorrow's complex, uncertain, and dangerous world. This does not, however, mean such sharing will be easy to arrange.

MAASTRICHT AND THE NEW EUROPE

Is Europe as a full partner of the United States the dream of a few visionaries following in Jean Monnet's footsteps or a realistic goal to be attained in the foreseeable future? The answer is only tangentially dependent on the United States. It will primarily be determined by the ability of the EC member countries to transform their nearly completed economic community into a political community. Such was the ambitious goal of the summit held on December 10 and 11, 1991, in Maastricht—a goal that was only partially attained. The Maastricht agreements drafted at the summit and signed on February 7, 1992, heralded an important stage in European construction. They do not, however, go far enough to allow for the emergence of the European pillar needed in transatlantic relations. More progress and more agreements are necessary. The Maastricht agreements are nonetheless deserving of careful study, if only because of the great impact they will have on the relations between the United States and Europe.

One preliminary observation: German reunification has not, as some predicted, sounded the death knell of European construction. On the contrary, the process has been accelerated. Germany has not turned away from the Community to escape the limitations it imposes and launch, on its own, a winner-takes-all strategy for postcommunist Europe. At the same time,

Germany's partners have not let themselves be slowed down
by the fear that Germany would dominate the Community's
structures. Obviously, a reunified Germany freed from the
threat to its security presented by the Soviet arsenal has new
weight in Europe. This was shown when it increased the interest rate in 1991, and again when it recognized Slovenia and
Croatia. This disturbed some people on both sides of the Atlantic, but it would be incorrect to overdramatize the situation.
The nationalist tendencies that may be observed in Germany,
and elsewhere, did not lead Germany to drag its feet at
Maastricht. On the contrary, Chancellor Helmut Kohl was the
most determined advocate of European integration. It was England that put on the brakes, abetted in some areas, such as
an increase in power for Parliament or the Commission, by
France.

The progress that the Maastricht agreements have brought
about in European construction has occurred on two levels:
economic and political. Most of the progress has been made
in the monetary field, where advances have been decisive. The
commitments made and deadlines agreed upon are so precise
and so binding that the move toward monetary union may be
held to be irreversible. For this to become possible, several
conditions had to be met.

—The future monetary union's mechanisms, beginning with
the future European Central Bank's membership, powers, and
independence had to be very precisely defined; and this they
were, down to the slightest detail.

—The decision to move to a single currency had to be
defined to require, not unanimity, but a majority decision by
the Community's members; and so it shall be.

—The European currency had to be able to come into being
even if, when the time came, all twelve countries did not satisfy
the rigorous conditions laid down on balanced budgets, stable
prices, and deficits; it was so decided.

—Finally, precise deadlines had to be set forth, and so they were. Monetary union can come into force as early as January 1, 1997, if seven of the twelve countries are willing and able. If not, and no other date is set by the end of 1997, union will occur on January 1, 1999.

These decisions are not merely economic in scope. They are also political to a very great extent. A single currency requires convergent fiscal and tax choices and, therefore, an inevitable rapprochement of government policies in all fields. The single currency will be an irresistible union accelerator.

Only one question remains open on the transition to monetary union after Maastricht: the influence of business-cycle uncertainty, which must not be underestimated. There is a real possibility that the recession, if it continues and worsens, may lead the Community's member countries to implement divergent policies, loose in some countries—Italy, Great Britain, France, and Benelux—and tight in others, such as Germany and the Netherlands. If this were to happen, the introduction of a common currency could be delayed. But the determination of member states, particularly France and Germany, to respect the stipulated deadlines is so great that this eventuality may be considered highly unlikely.

The political component of the Maastricht agreements is comparatively modest. The decisions of principle are ambitious, and the declarations of intent resounding. Concrete commitments or binding rules, however, will be sought for in vain.

The Community's member states declare themselves determined to implement common foreign and defense policies. The day this commitment is upheld will certainly mark an immense step forward toward a federal Europe. However, the provisions made for implementation give scant grounds for optimism. Foreign policy will, in fact, continue to be determined through traditional intergovernmental cooperation and not through the Community's much more effective procedures and institutions set up by the Treaty of Rome. In particular, this means that decisions will continue to require unanimity. Under such conditions, nothing guarantees that the Community's member states will show greater unity and a stronger will in the future, or that they will be able to mobilize more considerable means than they did for the Gulf War or the Yugoslav crisis.

On the other hand, certain provisions are more daring. Such is the case of the joint-action procedure established by the Maastricht agreements, a new procedure whose principles, goals, means, duration, and implementation could require only a qualified majority. This is a considerable measure of progress, but the precautions taken are so limiting that doubt is cast on the probability that the Community's member states will have frequent recourse to such joint action.

The Maastricht agreements further stipulate that defense, for which no authority had until now been vested in the Community, shall henceforth be included in the Community's sphere of competence. This decision is of paramount importance for the future, but so far it has had only one consequence for the member states: entrusting the Western European Union with the Community's military affairs and transferring its headquarters from London to Brussels.

The practical consequences of this decision will largely depend on the United States. None of the Community's member states, and France no more than the rest, in fact wishes to provoke or accelerate America's disengagement from Europe. The Maastricht agreements unambiguously state that nothing will be done which might negatively affect NATO. It will therefore be up to the United States to reflect upon the extent and form of its future military commitments in Europe. If these were to be reduced to a symbolic presence in the foreseeable future, it would be better for Washington to rapidly draw the necessary conclusions concerning NATO's structure and the role that the Community's member states will be called upon to play within NATO. Europe is psychologically ready to assume its defense responsibilities, but a true European defense pillar will only come to be when the United States gives the signal and on condition that the new structures do not weaken the coupling of the two shores of the Atlantic, to which the Old World is as deeply attached as it has always been.

In this context, Great Britain's attitude is of obvious importance. Moreover, the reservations Britain expressed at Maastricht concerning both monetary union and the social provisions of the agreements cast doubt, if not on the sincerity of Britain's European commitment, at least on the idea that Britain will one day adhere to Germany and France's federal conception of the Europe of the future. However, Britain has come somewhat closer to this concept in the last two decades, and Prime Minister John Major's position at Maastricht was partly dictated by electoral considerations. It is therefore likely that Great Britain will ultimately choose not to isolate itself from the Continent and end up supporting, willingly or otherwise, France and Germany's initiatives. It is, however, certain that this development will be all the faster and freer of mental reservations if the United States also chooses to encourage and rely upon the European process.

It must be emphasized that this process involves one unknown factor that should not be ignored: the probability that the Community will be broadened to include Scandinavia and Eastern Europe. The ink on the Maastricht agreements will hardly have time to dry before the negotiations for Sweden's and Austria's accession to the Community begin, in turn inciting Poland, Czechoslovakia, and Hungary to step up the pressure to be admitted themselves. This gives rise to one further question: are the structures the Community forged for itself at Maastricht strong enough to bear the trauma of these successive enlargements? There can be no doubt about the answer. It is clearly in the negative.

If the Community's member countries wish to maintain and develop the ability to decide and to act that they have begun to acquire and at the same time open their doors to new members, they will first of all have to undertake a thoroughgoing reform of the Community's institutions. They will have to give the Community executive powers worthy of the name, generalize majority voting, and explore ways and means of allowing the more resolute to stride forward without being paralyzed by more timid or weaker members, and all this without weakening the Community. The challenge is formidable. But Europe will become a credible partner for the United States and Japan only if it rises to the challenge.

CONCLUSION

When facing the shock waves the collapse of the Soviet system and empire are causing to spread through Europe and beyond, two attitudes are possible.

The first would be to preserve, to the greatest extent possible, the structures set up to resist communist expansionism, adapting them where necessary. These structures have proved to work. It is to be hoped they could be used for other purposes. This is the prudent approach.

The other attitude would be to take as a starting point the changes that have occurred and derive from them a new architecture better adapted to the demands of the present and future. This is the ambitious approach. What European and international order might it bring about? It would be premature to attempt to decide. But the hypothesis might be put forward that this order would not be, as some have claimed, a unipolar one, given the United States' lack of the political will and economic resources necessary to play policeman of the world on its own, nor would it be an authentically multipolar one, since America's military supremacy will assure it the role of first among equals for a long time to come.

A mixed system seems likelier. It would resemble a directorate of continents, acting under the legal and moral cover of the United Nations and under the effective direction of the United States. But if such a directorate of continents is to see the light of day and to find acceptance, Europe will need to be represented, not in the traditional fragmented guise to which the world is accustomed, but rather as a homogeneous, united whole upon which the United States and Japan may lean and from which they may, when appropriate, seek assistance. One of the goals of U.S. foreign policy could and should be to contribute to the birth of its European partner.

Michael Stürmer

5

Germany in Search of an Enlightened American Leadership

G ERMAN REUNIFICATION and its wider implications ended forty years of the Cold War. For better or worse, this will not only affect U.S.-German relations in the decade to come by placing them in a widely different strategic setting but also change the rules and the unspoken assumptions of the transatlantic relationship.

The differences between German unity in the mid-nineteenth century and German unity at the end of the twentieth century are fundamental. The most obvious difference is that after 1848 Bismarck staged a Prussian revolution from above and brought unity to Germany through a series of duel-like wars, with the United States engaged in retrenchment and reform at home and Britain uneasily attending the old and new balance of the European system. In 1990 German unity was part of the disintegration of the Soviet Union's outer empire, and the process was imbedded in a comprehensive negotiating process, including much summitry, carefully guided, orchestrated, and super-

vised by the United States. At the same time the United States
redefined its own role in Europe as not only the traditional
"balance from beyond the sea" but also the power giving
reassurance to Germans and non-Germans alike. The question
remains whether the two countries, Germany and the United
States, will respond to the pressures of world management
together or drift apart under the spell of the new freedom they
seem to have won now that the Cold War is over. If these two
countries are unable or unwilling to act in concert, there is
little chance to give shape and meaning to anything resembling
a new world order.

It is worth recalling that under Bismarck and after Bismarck
Germany was forever too small for hegemony and too large
for balance, unable to define itself and its European environment. Today the Atlantic is the new Mediterranean, the United
States and Germany the two centers of gravity, though with a
different *modus operandi*, different means at their disposal,
and different relationships with the past and the future. If in
the nineteenth century Germany was left with the fundamental
ambiguity of its geostrategic situation in the center of the European system, both a predicament and a temptation, Germany
is all but geographically an Atlantic power and part of the
West's maritime alliance. To the east of Germany there is
nothing but the precariousness of the countries coming in from
the cold, and to the east of them looms nothing but the post-
Soviet chaos.

Still, the concern voiced by the Tory leader Benjamin Disraeli in the British House of Commons in early 1871 could
also have come from one of his successors 120 years later:

> The German revolution, a greater political event than the French
> revolution of last century. . . . Not a single principle in the man-
> agement of our foreign affairs, accepted by all statesmen for guid-
> ance up to six months ago, any longer exists. There is not a
> diplomatic tradition which has not been swept away. You have a

new world, new influences at work, new and unknown objects
and dangers with which to cope, at present involved in that ob-
scurity incident to novelty in such affairs.[1]

In the time of Disraeli there was still a European system,
which ever since the Congress of Vienna was centered around
Germany in its various forms. This system broke down in the
two world wars of the twentieth century and was literally wiped
out in the Cold War. But the Cold War has ended; the configuration and the mechanics of the world have changed beyond
recognition. History is being remembered. In the West, necessity has given way to choice. Alliances long regarded as a
lifeline tend to be regarded in terms of cost-benefit analysis.
Old loyalties are being tested by the convenience of conflicting
national interests. The transatlantic bargain in general, and the
German-American partnership in particular, are undergoing
change. And this transformation will be enhanced by what is
happening in the East: the Soviet Union is no more, the new
"Commonwealth" is nothing but an agreement to disagree,
and nobody can tell what in the long run will replace the last
of the great empires. What is certain, however, is that the
decline and fall of the Soviet empire will cause shifts and
changes, eruptions and power struggles on a scale that may
remind the world of the long decline and the painful agonies
of the Spanish empire, the Ottoman empire, and the Austro-
Hungarian monarchy.

Next to U.S. containment Soviet pressure served as the main
federator of Europe and the Atlantic alliance in the immediate
postwar era. The brutal divide between East and West helped
to integrate Germans into the European system and, indeed,
into the global trade and monetary system for the first time in
modern German history. The West Germans, at least, paid the
price of national partition without shedding too many tears
about unity lost, leaving it to the East Germans to continue
losing the Second World War for another forty years. The

bipolar system had the additional effect of providing much discipline, calm, and oil whenever the waves of the Atlantic Ocean were surging high. By now, that system has given way to differences dictated by national interest over how to handle Eastern Europe's misery, how to manage the crises and conflicts of the Soviet Union's succession, and how to bail out the newly emerging democracies and semidemocracies of the former Eastern bloc. That is now a world in transit, threatened by its old demons and still living under the shadow of what Winston Churchill once called "a riddle wrapped in a mystery inside an enigma," that is, Russia.

The United States will continue to try to play the superpower duopoly with Russia: hence the long insistence on doing business with Gorbachev and no one else, on keeping the Union together, and on preserving central control over nuclear weapons and, after the 1991 coup, the attempt to create a privileged relationship with Boris Yeltsin's Russia, the chief heir—but, alas, not the only one—to the former Soviet Union's arsenal of mass destruction. Germany sees its security linked to watertight arms control–cum–verification agreements reaching out to the Urals; the United States would be more inclined to accept unilateral understandings. Whatever the outcome, there must be an intimate division of labor, and economic benefits should not be given without large concessions in the arms-control field.

The United States is no longer forced into global confrontation but can deal with crises one by one—or not at all. In the Gulf War, the United States threw almost everything into battle; in the Adriatic, the U.S. Sixth Fleet was conspicuous by its absence. In the future, the Europeans will find it more difficult than in the past to predict the movements of a reluctant world leader. Containment of the Soviet Union was indeed successful beyond expectation, deterrence kept the Soviets at arm's length, and reassurance helped to reorganize Western Europe. But since there is no more Soviet threat—only a post-

Soviet chaos, coupled with "instability and uncertainty"—can the beneficial effects of the Cold War, calculability and alliance coherence, be reinvented?

In one way or the other, the United States and Western Europe will have to make a deliberate effort to create new foundations and new forms for an alliance that—for both sides—continues to be essential. The Soviet succession, the Islamic arc of crisis, proliferation, and people's migration will be on the world agenda, and they will, in their mutual interdependence, overtax any nation's capacity to respond adequately on its own. This agenda cannot be dealt with except in concert.

My argument is that the United States and Germany will be key actors in the world of the 1990s—with Germany the chief promoter of European economic and monetary union and political union, and the United States the last superpower, but one without a desire to confront and one no longer willing and able to carry the burden. The United States, however, continues to be needed in Europe as the balance from beyond the sea, and the alliance will also help the United States to define its long-term role in the current state of uncertainty, which may not be the serene epilogue to the Cold War but merely a wild prologue to the new world disorder. But to make the alliance the basis of cooperation, the Germans would have to provide more than money—in particular, methodology and a long-term vision—and the United States, a strategic umbrella and political reassurance.

THE UNITED STATES LIBERATED OF THE COLD WAR

The French philosopher and strategic thinker Raymond Aron once noted that in times of fundamental change the content of governments' secret dossiers matters less than the history and culture of nations. The United States may not be an exception to this rule. America invented itself as the new world while it never ceased to wish to recreate the old world in its own image. To thank God for the protection offered by two surrounding oceans against the tribulations of the rest of the world while wishing to make the world safe for democracy has been the fundamental ambivalence governing American foreign policy in the twentieth century. This ambivalence has made U.S. foreign policy less than predictable for friend and foe alike—the last forty years being a long exception—and it has created an unspoken fear among Americans that they might miss, whatever course they choose, their manifest destiny.

Obviously, the present readjustment of U.S. foreign policy and its domestic support has been caused by the breakdown of the Soviet Union and the end of the Cold War. The U.S. strategic community looks at the post-Soviet chaos with mixed feelings; the rest of the country celebrates what looks like the triumph of American values, which has led to a surrealistic debate on "the end of history" in 1991 and a scramble for the peace dividend. The material reasons are to be found in Russia, the psychological motives in America.

When at the time of the Napoleonic wars Thomas Jefferson, in his First Inaugural Address, warned his fellow Americans against engaging in "entangling alliances" with European powers, this showed not only diplomatic prudence but also fear of being contaminated by the old evils of European power plays. Later in the nineteenth century Alexis de Tocqueville looked at the imperial republic and observed a deep-rooted lack of interest in the theory of foreign policy and a bad conscience over its practice. In the course of the twentieth century the United States decided about balance and hegemony in Europe no less than three times: in 1917, in 1944, and in 1948. After forty years of guarding the banks of the Elbe, is there a promised land, once again, called "America first"?

There is no shortage of leaders and prophets favoring ''America first.'' The Republicans who in 1920 forced the United States to retreat from Europe have been converted to globalism only under the impact of the Soviet threat, and under the leadership of Nixon, Reagan, and Bush. The Democrats, out to make the world safe for democracy in World War I and to contain Soviet expansionism after World War II, are now more inward looking. Both parties since the mid-1980s have engaged in a deep reorientation process, and the result could be a U.S. policy that refuses to provide balance, leadership, and reassurance for the rest of the world. If that happens, the ''new world order,'' proclaimed in early 1991, would be nothing but a way of speaking.

The Republicans might try to find their own isolationist roots; the Democrats, Roosevelt's New Deal and Johnson's Great Society. U.S. leaders will try to redefine America's destiny; they may not find it in the CSCE (Conference on Security and Cooperation in Europe) world from Vancouver via Vienna to Vladivostok or beyond, but somewhere between the state of California and the state of Maine via the Midwest.

However, if America refused a role in the destinies of Europe, or retired in bitterness, the old world would not be a happy place. The United States, meanwhile, would lose, along with its wider engagements, part of its belief in itself and, indeed, much of its self-respect. Sooner or later, however, the last of the superpowers would have to leave the psychologist's couch and stand up in order to lend muscle to the new world order proudly proclaimed and sadly neglected. At the end of the twentieth century it is both America's privilege and predicament that it cannot escape its role as leader of the West.

''Containment of Soviet expansionist tendencies,'' to quote the Sovietologist George F. Kennan, became the leitmotif of U.S. foreign policy in 1947. What happened forty years later was what far-sighted architects had expected: the mellowing of Soviet power, the retreat of the Soviet army, the decline and fall of the last of the great land empires. In this way, after 1945 the United States continued the "Europe first" policy that had determined the grand strategy of the Second World War. It was the power of the United States that saved the Europeans the pain of repeating their history and arming themselves against one another. This policy was translated into the Atlantic alliance, with wide implications. The economic integration of Europe was not only approved by the United States but in fact facilitated by it, as Washington, through the Marshall Plan, saved the Europeans from the zero-sum game of the 1920s while, through its nuclear superpower, allowing them to keep the military burden relatively minor.

But today the United States is worried about itself more than about the outside world. And this, as seen from outside, is less than reassuring. Fundamental cultural changes and shifts are under way, especially in the American South and West. The debate over curricula at schools and universities, over whether Shakespeare and other "dead white old men" have something to say that Americans should listen to, reveals uncertainties and the search for a new direction. The melting pot was destined to produce a white Anglo-Saxon Protestant alloy. Today, however, the Stars and Stripes are fluttering over an ethnic puzzle. The legal system still carries the marks of its historic origin, the Constitution is an expression of European enlightenment, and the architecture from Harvard Quadrangle to the Capitol is European Palladianism—but maybe all these will soon be sentimental values.

But why not, after forty years, thank the Americans and wish them well on their way home? Looking at German unification and its European conditions, one cannot escape the conclusion that in the future America will have to take up once again the role of balancer in Europe that England, throughout the nineteenth century, exercised so masterfully. Any look at Poland and territories to the south and east should remind everybody why the presence of the United States is being urgently desired in that area. And whoever considers the vast arsenal of Soviet nuclear weapons, 27,000 or more, cannot escape the conclusion that a nuclear superpower, even more so in decay, needs a nuclear superpower on the other side. Nonproliferation virtue will give way to proliferation vice, nuclear weapons being dictators' drugs. There is a need for world order and European crisis management that cannot be satisfied without having America in the driver's seat.

America's future role cannot be the abstract result of outdated scenarios of the Cold War. But it is important that America's place is understood as that of continuing to be the centerpiece of world stability. That is why Germany and the United States need to formulate a new transatlantic arrangement. In this, Europe will count not so much for its military potential but rather for its conceptual and political cohesion and for whether it can make itself essential to the long-term security and interests of the United States. Here Germany has more to contribute than most Germans, their leaders included, would accept after the successful conclusion of the Cold War, above all a willingness to take part in painful decisions and their implementation.

GERMANY: A COUNTRY IN SEARCH OF AN ENLIGHTENED NATIONAL INTEREST

Germany after World War II was recreated in America's image. In 1990 President George Bush guided German unification through the troubled waters of European and world politics. But both countries run a risk of misreading the next chapter. For the United States, the rationale of the new world order—to fight "instability and insecurity"—may not be enough to convince Congress and Middle America. For Germany, the retreat of the Russians could be misunderstood as a signal that the U.S. mission has been fulfilled and, even more, that the country's destiny is to be found in the middle of Europe; instead, Germany may find itself, after some time, abandoned in the middle of nowhere.

When, in the 1960s, Henry Kissinger visited Bonn, he was led to observe that Germany was different from any other major ally of the United States: "Defeated in two wars, bearing the stigma of the Nazi past, dismembered and divided, West Germany was an economy in search of political purpose. . . . The Federal Republic was like an imposing tree with shallow roots, vulnerable to sudden gusts of wind."[2] Kissinger's heroic pessimism was not borne out by subsequent events. Reunification required a keen sense of international bargaining and domestic management of power. However, after unification Germany is still in the process of forming a national interest—and is frightened by having to do so. But the process is inevitable. It can succeed only if both Germany and the United States pursue, though under vastly different circumstances, the substance of their alliance and understand their difficult but inescapable interdependence.

At the turn of the century, when both the United States and Germany put in a bid for world power, the two countries turned into rivals, and twice Germany's land-bound empire had to succumb to the U.S.-led maritime alliance. All postwar history has taught the Germans that their currencies of powers are of a nonmilitary kind. In fact, the country created the Bundeswehr not as a return to its bad old ways but as its "defense contribution," *contre-coeur*, and as its membership card for the Western club. The Bundeswehr was meant to deter; it was never meant to fight. Hence the present state of shock at seeing the world go out of joint and having to think about the implications for Germany's innocence—and convenience. But

Germans and Americans have different ways of addressing their isolationism.

It was without any visible regret that Chancellor Konrad Adenauer renounced production and possession of modern atomic, biological, and chemical weapons in 1954 to reassure the French and other European neighbors that Germany had mended her ways. In 1990, when Germany's continuing nonnuclear status became a condition of Soviet assent to the German unification accord, not even a debate ensued inside Germany, let alone serious controversy. Provided the country does not suddenly see itself seriously threatened from outside and seriously abandoned by the United States and the other NATO allies, there will be no call or constituencies for a return to the military expression of power. The Gulf War, when Germany was so hesitant to face the grim reality of aggression and retribution, was a moment of truth for the country. It awoke to the fact that war is feasible in the post–Cold War world, and it lost some of its innocence on the way—as well as a lot of money and military hardware.

But for the foreseeable future Germany will rather face bitter criticism from its allies for being too soft than face its own memories and those of others for being too tough. In matters military and strategic Germany will return to its pre-Bismarckian habit of trying to organize itself and its environment more by consensus and compromise than by the sword. So, in matters of "blood and iron" the country will be extremely reluctant to police the world, not even in conjunction with others. The surrealistic debate on a nonexistent clause in the *Grundgesetz* (the Constitution) that would stop Germany from taking part in collective defense, and the unwarranted interpretation of NATO's out-of-area concept, should reassure the world that it is too little the West can expect from Germany rather than too much. No imperial rival to the United States, no ambitious competitor, will emerge, but at best a junior partner.

In this context, German attitudes toward Europe fail to pro-

vide a key. Chancellor Helmut Kohl, together with President
François Mitterrand, suggested that German unification should
result not only in a larger Germany but also in a more effective
Europe. Hence the two Intergovernmental Conferences of
1991, the Maastricht summit, and the resolve to create a single
European currency and an integrated European defense identity. In the Franco-German alliance this new departure had
been prepared for by both the invention of a Franco-German
army corps—the Germans NATO-assigned, the French, of
course, not—and the upgrading of the Western European
Union, always the sleeping beauty, to a new status as the
missing link between NATO and the European Community.
Unfortunately the Germans thought they were bringing France
back into NATO, while the French believed they had decisively
created the first part of a French-led European army. The com-
plications will not end here. So far, Germany's self-inflicted
constitutional inhibitions have not been sorted out, and at present no contingency can be imagined that would meet the requirements to allow the new corps to move.

Meanwhile, the French president raised the stakes by posing
the question whether it was not time to surround French nuclear
weapons with a European doctrine for European defense. In
Germany, however, this departure was greeted with less enthusiasm than the French had expected. First, a serious Euro-
defense would entangle Germany in many problems, especially
Mediterranean ones, that the country would not like, let alone
support. Second, the persuasive power of French nuclear weapons would enhance the weight of France in European politics.
Third, the French idea would increase the risk of the United
States abandoning the old continent—thus pushing Germany
even more into the dreaded direction of having to look after
its own security, even ''out of area.'' Finally, there is no way
that French nuclear weapons, which lack the subtle technology
as well as the strategic reconnaissance U.S. weapons are as-

sociated with, could seriously take over the role of the U.S. potential. In the end, after much enthusiasm in Germany has been displayed, it will discover that the problems of the *"ménage à trois"* persist and that the strategic alliance with the North Americans must be preserved—if necessary at the cost of many European illusions.

In the years ahead, a strong argument can also be made for Germany to display leadership in the GATT and handle U.S. interests with care, especially the American sensitivities about free trade and fair trade. For the time being, Germany, together with the United Kingdom, is the main European force for free trade, even if some not inconsiderable flaws must be admitted, such as the Common Agricultural Policy of the Community. But Germany will have to be the advocate of trade liberalism not merely to do the United States a favor or give a chance to the young democracies in Eastern Europe, which have so little else to offer on the world market. As the workshop of the world, Germany has a vested interest in keeping Western Europe on the narrow path of economic virtue, and it will be unable to do so without the strong and guiding influence of the United States.

United Germany will find its political role in Europe and vis-à-vis the post-Soviet uncertainties only if and when the politicians, like the public at large, understand and accept the vital importance of the Atlantic alliance with the United States. Chances are they will do so, but this cannot be a unilateral NATO that relies exclusively on U.S. leadership. The United States, in turn, will be able to strike a new transatlantic bargain only if and when it accepts the ambiguity of the new, post–Cold War situation: that America is still needed in Europe as the great balancer beyond the sea, the provider of reassurance, and the nuclear lender of last resort, while Europe develops its own economic and political agenda and furnishes itself with the institutional wherewithal.

CONCLUSION: AN ENTANGLING ALLIANCE

The U.S. involvement in Europe was immensely successful in the past. It is undergoing profound change, but it will have to survive in substance. In Europe the agenda of the Cold War is over. But it would be tragic if the Atlantic nations misunderstood the fragility of the world in transition. The United States still has responsibilities and interests in Europe, both visible and invisible. It will have to balance nuclear power by nuclear power. It will have to be, beyond the military sphere, the team leader in managing the Soviet succession and limiting the chaotic implications. The old fears and nightmares of European nations both East and West cannot be put to rest while the United States goes into imperial retirement. Together with Germany the United States will have to insist on free trade in the councils of the industrial democracies. Germany will ask the United States for two things: to support the effort to save Eastern Europe from the postcommunist abyss and to continue to be the nuclear lender of last resort.

The United States is, to cite the title of Joseph Nye's book, "bound to lead." But the Europeans must understand that post–Cold War America has a grim agenda waiting at home and that cooperation will be valued and friends will be counted. Part two of the Pax Americana will be a joint venture, or it will not take place. Both sides must remember that peace continues to have a price, that alliances are not free of charge, and that no viable option is available.

NOTES

1. See W. F. Monypenny and G. E. Buckle, *The Life of Benjamin Disraeli*, vol. 2 (London, 1929), p. 473.
2. Henry Kissinger, *White House Years* (Little, Brown, 1979), p. 97.

Leonhard Gleske

6

The Opportunities and Perils for the United States of European Integration

F INANCIAL, MONETARY, AND ECONOMIC AFFAIRS are playing an important role in the creation of a new Europe and in its relationship with the United States. The construction of a European economic and monetary union, with, in its final stage, a single European currency replacing the existing national currencies and a European System of Central Banks, firmly committed to price stability as its primary objective and in sole charge of the European Community's common monetary policy, will introduce a major new force into the world economic order.

In the remarks that follow I first consider the political and economic implications of European monetary integration and describe the German position in this regard, then turn to the question of the prospective impact of European monetary union on Europe's economic and monetary relations with the United States.

DEVELOPMENT OF THE COMMON MARKET

The Common Market, whose membership has gradually grown from the original six countries to twelve, was created primarily with the aim of close economic integration. However, when they first concluded the treaty establishing the European Coal and Steel Community and then created the Common Market under the Treaty of Rome, the European statesmen of the 1950s always had in mind the much more far-reaching objective of political integration. The final objective has always been political. Jean Monnet, the most eminent of the Community's founding fathers, realized that the political goal could be reached only by a high degree of economic integration. A customs union and a single market were never considered the final objective. The goal of completing the Common Market by the end of 1992 and the great political will engaged in developing it further into a European monetary union have again made clear the close connection between economic and political integration.

Monetary policy questions were important from the earliest days of the Common Market, as well as in the negotiations on the Treaty of Rome. Indeed, a "common market" in the true sense of the term must be described as incomplete and imperfect so long as it comprises different currencies that are, moreover, linked by changing parities. The further development of the Common Market, culminating in a monetary union or, even better, a single currency and thus an indivisible monetary policy for which an institution at the Community level would have to be responsible—all this was therefore inherent in the logic of the process of European integration set in motion in the 1950s. However, this logical progression was not reflected—or not strongly enough reflected—in the Treaty of Rome itself.

Significant aspects of general economic policy—trade policy

vis-à-vis third countries and agricultural policy in particular—
became issues to be dealt with at the Community level; the
member countries transferred their responsibilities in these
areas to Community bodies. International trade agreements are
thus no longer concluded by the individual member states, nor
are the preparatory negotiations conducted by them. These are
matters for the Community institutions, that is, the Council of
Ministers and the European Commission. This situation also
applies to the GATT negotiations. The negotiating party is now
the Community, not the member states. The process of reaching
consensus within the Community is difficult owing to the
sometimes differing interests and economic policy aims of the
individual member countries. The negotiations in the so-called
Uruguay Round, in particular with respect to agricultural protectionism, have therefore not always been easy.

In other areas of economic policy, member states committed
themselves to closer coordination. Monetary policy, however,
remained the sole responsibility and sovereign right of the
individual member countries. The Treaty of Rome requires
them to cooperate in the field of monetary policy only to the
extent that this is necessary for the smooth functioning of the
Common Market, a notion that has never been defined precisely. The member countries were to consider exchange-rate
policy a matter of common interest, but it remained entirely
in the national sphere of competence. The reason for this ret-
icence in the monetary policy area lay in the fact that a transfer
of monetary responsibilities to bodies at the Community level
would have had far-reaching political implications for the sovereignty of the member countries. The attitude of the United
Kingdom—but not only of that country—toward a European
monetary union shows that such concerns persist undiminished
even today.

In the history of the European Community there have been
a number of attempts to establish a monetary union or at least

a "zone of monetary stability." The most successful of these—
though its ambitions did not extend to a full monetary union—
was the establishment of the European Monetary System
(EMS) in 1979. The then president of France, Valéry Giscard
d'Estaing, and the chancellor of West Germany, Helmut
Schmidt, were the architects of this system, which, after it had
been given realistic shape in negotiations among the central
banks concerned, proved to be a great success despite the many
doubts that had existed at its inception. Ultimately, however,
this success was due less to the mechanics of the system, whose
disciplinary effects have at times been exaggerated, than to the
entirely autonomous decisions of its members to pursue an
economic and monetary policy geared primarily to domestic
price stability and, in the context of such a policy—and not
least in support of it—to tie their currencies to the deutsche
mark. That currency over the years had become by far the most
stable currency in the Common Market and was also the currency of the member country with the greatest economic
weight.

As a result of these autonomous decisions of the other member countries, the Bundesbank, as the institution responsible
for the deutsche mark, unintentionally and indeed somewhat
reluctantly assumed a dominant role within the European Monetary System. The monetary policy decisions of the Bundesbank have also increasingly become a determining factor for
the conduct of monetary policy in the other EMS member
countries. It is therefore understandable that for some Community governments and central banks the development toward
a monetary union is also seen as a means of participating in
the monetary policy decisionmaking process rather than being
exposed to the consequences of monetary policy measures decided independently by the Bundesbank.

The success of the European Monetary System was undoubtedly a decisive factor behind the initiative to complete the

Common Market by the end of 1992. The dynamism thereby triggered was in turn the main motivation for reviving the old and previously unfruitful ideas regarding monetary union and for pushing ahead with them with, as it appears, a stronger political impetus than in the past.

THE POLITICAL SIDE OF MONETARY UNION

The essential ingredient of a monetary union is the irrevocable fixing of exchange rates between the currencies of the countries belonging to it. In economic terms, that is tantamount to having a single currency. To this extent, the transition to a single currency for the whole area of the monetary union would therefore be of little economic importance, provided the fixing of exchange rates was viewed by the markets as definitive and credible. But the transition to a single currency would be of great symbolic and hence also political significance. After all, in economic terms, it would of course imply that the decision to establish monetary union would no longer be called into question, as it could well be if national currencies continued to exist.

The decision to enter into a monetary union and to renounce the right to change the exchange rate once and for all will have far-reaching political implications for each country. Countries will no longer be able to insulate their economies from external developments and influences running counter to their own economic and monetary policy objectives. Fundamental powers in the area of monetary and exchange-rate policy will have to be exercised at the Community level. Each member state will of course participate in the decisionmaking process within the institutions set up for this purpose, in particular a European System of Central Banks, but it will no longer have sovereign authority over such decisions.

In a unified currency area monetary policy cannot be decided
at the national level. National autonomy in the field of monetary
and exchange-rate policy will cease to exist. National monetary
policies will need to be replaced by a common monetary policy
for the whole currency area, together with an institution having
responsibility for it. This requirement was already clearly stated
in the Werner Report at the beginning of the 1970s, when the
Community member states undertook their first—albeit unsuc-
cessful—attempt to establish a monetary union, and recently
once again in the Delors Report.

But there are other political implications, too. Monetary,
fiscal, and general economic policies cannot be conducted sep-
arately from one another; each has to be compatible with the
others. That raises the questions whether, and to what extent,
the powers and responsibilities of the Community at the leg-
islative and executive levels need to be extended, and what
institutional arrangements are required to safeguard this com-
patibility. So far the answers to these questions have not been
as unambiguous as in the case of monetary policy itself. Budgetary policy, in particular, presents difficulties. Opinions on
how far and in what way budgetary policy should be subject
to the influence of Community institutions still differ widely.

And finally, the decision to establish a monetary union with
irrevocably fixed exchange rates or even a single currency does
not mean an end to the problems that now take the form of
balance-of-payments and exchange-rate problems. They then
change their nature and in a monetary union become problems
of regional imbalances. In a unified economic area whose parts
are interlinked by fixed exchange rates, locational disadvan-
tages or structural shifts between regions due, for example, to
external shocks can no longer be offset by exchange-rate
changes. Such problems of regional imbalances are exacerbated
when locational factors are not offset by flexibility and regional
differentiation in wages and other costs, as they are to a great

extent in the United States, where there is also a remarkable degree of labor mobility.

In the course of a long political process, de facto mechanisms to compensate for interregional imbalances have been created in all the industrial countries. One such mechanism is a large central budget, which has regional redistributive effects similar to those of the national social security and unemployment insurance systems. To illustrate, in the United States it is estimated that no less than 40 percent of the decline in income in the state of Texas caused by the fall in oil prices in the mid-1980s and the resulting recession was offset by lower payments of federal taxes and higher federal expenditure in favor of Texas in the form of unemployment benefits and welfare payments. And in Germany, for example, there is a so-called horizontal fiscal adjustment between fiscally weak and fiscally strong Länder, aimed at ensuring approximately comparable living standards.

Similar mechanisms for evening out interregional imbalances exist only in embryo at a Community level. Compared with the Community's size, its budget is very small, and the structural and regional funds, even though they have gained in importance, also play a minor role in this regard. Overcoming these imbalances by means of large-scale financial transfers, as is being demanded by Spain, for example, with support from others, could perhaps place excessive demands on the political willingness and solidarity of the member countries. The undoubtedly extreme, but for this reason typical, example of monetary integration in a unified Germany illustrates the extent of the problem that might arise if the step toward monetary union in Europe is taken while there is still a lack of convergence.

Entering on a monetary union is not only an economic step; it also implies entering a community based on solidarity, in which the stronger members are willing to support the weaker members with voluntary contributions. For Germany, this willingness could be taken for granted, given the objective of political reunification and the nation's feeling of solidarity. But we are still a long way from that point in Europe. In other words, the political integration of Europe must go hand in hand with economic and monetary integration. In the absence of political union, economic and monetary union will lack a firm foundation. That is why the question of "political union" arises in this context.

Any transfer of responsibilities to the Community in the different areas connected with monetary union requires an amendment to the Treaty of Rome. This was explicitly confirmed in the framework of the Single European Act of 1987 and the associated amendment to the treaty. Consequently, the content and form of any institutional changes have to be discussed in intergovernmental negotiations, and the treaty amending the Treaty of Rome then has to be ratified by the national parliaments in accordance with the respective national constitutional arrangements.

This procedure underlines the political significance of such a transfer of responsibility to Community bodies. It relates to fundamental areas of national sovereignty; namely, domestic monetary policy and exchange-rate policy vis-à-vis the outside world as well as fiscal policy, although much controversy still surrounds this last area. The intergovernmental conference on political union, convened at the same time as that on monetary union to discuss these wide-ranging political aspects of monetary union, fits into the overall picture.

Chancellor Helmut Kohl's insistence on political union is in keeping with the logic inherent in the process of monetary integration; it should not be interpreted as a bargaining maneuver. Germans are strongly convinced that a monetary union which is not based on political union, or at least accompanied by material progress in the direction of political union, would be doomed to failure. History demonstrates the truth of this

reasoning. The first national currencies in Europe were established in countries that had achieved political unity, such as
Great Britain, Sweden, and France. In such countries as Germany, Italy, and the United States, a national currency was
introduced only after the process of political unification was
complete. And conversely, in countries that, like the Soviet
Union and Yugoslavia, are breaking apart politically, one of
the first steps taken by member republics that want to loosen
their political ties to the central structure is to introduce their
own currency.

THE GERMAN POSITION

There is an additional dimension specific to the German political view of a European monetary union. The economic and
political development of western Germany since the 1950s and
the reunification of Germany in peace and freedom would not
have been possible without the Federal Republic's close ties
with the West, particularly in the absence of European integration. Without these close ties, a reunited Germany would
probably be as little in a position to cope with the major economic challenges posed by reunification as with the challenges
associated with the process of liberalization in central and eastern Europe. Monetary integration is also, and perhaps foremost,
a reflection of these close ties with the West. It is this percep-
tion that has led politicians in Germany not only to accept the
political consequences of monetary union but to see it as a
vehicle for political union. It is here that the attitude of responsible German politicians toward monetary union differs from
that of British politicians. We have no difficulty in agreeing
with our British friends in the analysis of the vast implications
of monetary union in Europe, but German politicians draw a
positive conclusion from it. They show a great willingness to

accept the consequences of monetary union in terms of loss of national sovereignty, provided of course that the agreement on monetary union meets fundamental requirements in terms of currency stability and the independence of a future European System of Central Banks.

Whatever the willingness to surrender sovereignty, however, the goal of European monetary union is not undisputed in Germany. Strong reservations arise from the fear that economic, fiscal, and monetary policies in a future monetary union will not be geared to the objective of domestic price stability in the same way as they are in Germany. In Germany such policies are founded on a broad underlying consensus. After the experience of two waves of inflation within a single generation, and their economic and political consequences, a consensus is not surprising. In most European countries, the will to pursue a policy of domestic monetary stability has also undoubtedly grown stronger, not least as a result of their own experiences in the 1970s. This change in attitude as well as appropriate policies has contributed significantly to the fact that the European Monetary System has functioned increasingly as a zone of stability.

Doubts nevertheless remain about whether this European consensus on the priority of price stability will withstand the trials ahead. If a future European monetary union were to be less resolute in pursuing this objective and if that were to result in higher inflation than has generally been experienced in Germany over the years, the direct advantages of a monetary union would soon be wiped out through the erosion of the value of financial assets. The tangible successes of an economic and social policy based on price stability would also be called into question.

Stable money—and I think this reflects the general conviction in Germany—is more important than a single currency. There is complete agreement between the federal government and the Bundesbank that the objective of German policy in all discussions within Community bodies and in the negotiations on a European monetary union is to establish the fundamental conditions for a monetary union geared to stability.

These conditions include:

—the commitment of a future European System of Central Banks to price stability as its primary objective;

—the institutional independence necessary for this commitment. The future European System of Central Banks should not be allowed to take instructions from national governments or from EC bodies. National central bank governors, who will sit on the European Central Bank's Council, must be independent of their governments;

—no financing of government budget deficits by the European System of Central Banks and strict limits on lending to the public sector; and

—closer and lasting convergence of national economic policies.

At their Maastricht summit meeting in December 1991 the Heads of State and Government of the EC countries reached broad agreement on these conditions. Together with the statute of the European System of Central Banks, with its strong commitment to price stability, these conditions form an important part of the Maastricht agreements.

The degree of convergence between the member states will determine when the final transition to monetary union can take place, that is, when exchange rates are fixed once and for all and the central banks of the member states transfer the monetary policy powers hitherto exercised nationally to a community institution, the European System of Central Banks. The degree of convergence, for which criteria have been defined, will also determine whether all member states can take this step at the same time. That would be politically desirable, but if it is not possible, the transition to monetary union will have to take place at different speeds.

The Heads of State and Government have proposed 1997

as the possible date of transition to monetary union. The intervening period is to be used to achieve the necessary convergence in terms of a sufficiently satisfactory degree of price stability, nonexcessive budget deficits, and a sustainable level of public debt. Before the end of 1996 the European Council will decide by qualified majority to launch European monetary union, provided that a simple majority of EC member states meets the convergence criteria, so that there is a "critical mass" of countries that can form the monetary union. If this critical mass is not reached at the end of 1996, monetary union will start at the beginning of 1999. The European Council will then only have to decide, again on a qualified majority basis, which member states fulfill the necessary conditions for the adoption of a single currency. To make the transition to monetary union irreversible, a protocol has been annexed to the treaty stipulating that no member state shall prevent entry into the monetary union.

In mid-1990 the Community embarked on "stage one" of the process leading to monetary union. This stage essentially differs little from the degree of monetary integration achieved hitherto in the European Monetary System. In the second stage, beginning in 1994, the first institutional step is to be taken, with the creation of a European Monetary Institute. Its task will be to promote and intensify monetary policy coordination and to prepare the ground for stage three. Opinions within the EC on the functions and responsibilities of this interim institution on the road to monetary union have differed widely. The initiators of the idea of setting up a monetary institution also considered that it should be given substantive monetary powers and should, for example, take over the task of influencing exchange-rate developments through intervention in the foreign exchange markets. However, that would have given rise to a gray area of monetary policy responsibility, which the German federal government and the Bundesbank were not prepared to accept.

Monetary policy is indivisible. It cannot accommodate a division of responsibilities between national and supranational institutions. It is thus clear that until the start of the final stage monetary policy responsibility in Germany will remain with the Bundesbank. The same applies for the other member states. The Bundesbank will therefore remain in charge of the fortunes of the deutsche mark and of monetary policy in Germany until the transfer of its monetary policy responsibilities to a European System of Central Banks, that is, at least until 1997. Since monetary policy responsibility is indivisible, this transfer cannot take place gradually but only in a single step. But creating the preconditions for such a decisive step—namely, the achievement of a satisfactory degree of convergence—is a gradual process that, it is hoped, a sufficiently large number of members of a future European monetary union will have taken part in by 1997.

EFFECTS OF EUROPEAN UNION
ON THE UNITED STATES

The process of European integration is an integral part of a broader development that will lead to a tripolar world economy, with the United States, the European Community, and Japan as the centers of gravity. Politically and economically the United States is now still the strongest power in the world, but the days of its solitary dominance, which characterized the world economy until the second half of the 1960s, are over. There is nothing surprising in that. In the long postwar period of peace and security, during which the United States took the lead in fostering and sustaining a framework that promoted political and economic stability, the formation of further centers of dynamic power was to be expected once the reconstruction of the European and Asian economies had been accomplished.

As a result of these developments, the relative economic

size of the largest industrial countries has changed considerably. At the beginning of the 1960s the share of the United States in world output was over 40 percent; it is now closer to 25 percent. The combined economy of the European Community is already slightly larger than that of the United States. On plausible assumptions concerning growth and exchange rates, the Japanese economy will reach three-quarters of U.S. gross national product by the year 2000. What is important in these relationships is that the three poles are already virtually identical in terms of openness to external events as defined by the ratio of foreign trade in goods and services to GNP.

The ascendancy of the U.S. economy in the Western world in the postwar period up to the mid-1960s was reflected in the importance of the U.S. dollar as a transactions, investment, and reserve currency. Although the international monetary system known as the Bretton Woods system had not been designed as such by its founding fathers, from the outset it was de facto a dollar standard. Directly or indirectly, almost all the members of this system tied their currencies to one another through a fixed relationship to the dollar. With a high level of domestic price stability stretching into the 1960s, the United States through its currency acted as the anchor of stability for the monetary system of the West.

However, the end of the period of reconstruction of the European and Asian economies coincided with a marked rise in U.S. inflation rates after the mid-1960s, thus bringing to a close the long period in which a domestically stable dollar had served usefully as an anchor for the whole international monetary system. Without the prerequisite of a stable dollar, the Bretton Woods system was bound to come to an end. In all probability, the change in relative positions within the world economy and the resulting reduction in the weight of the U.S. economy would anyway have had some impact on the role the dollar had assumed as a reserve and investment currency. But inflation in the United States caused the international role of the dollar to be impaired more than it would otherwise have been.

The international position of the dollar was, of course, never really in danger—in contrast to the experience of the pound sterling, which largely lost its status as a reserve currency in the 1960s. With a share in international reserves of close to 60 percent, the dollar is still by far the most important reserve currency and continues to be the key investment currency in the international financial markets. In both functions, however, the dollar now has to compete with other currencies. Monetary authorities and investors in general now have attractive alternatives from which to choose.

Once monetary union is complete, one of these alternatives will be a common European currency. In this respect it will take the place of the deutsche mark, which since the 1970s has become the second most important reserve currency after the dollar. Some 20 percent of global foreign exchange reserves are today held in deutsche marks, a sizable part of this amount by European central banks. The introduction—in 1997 at the earliest—of a European currency will undoubtedly lead to a restructuring of international foreign exchange reserves. But whether that will be at the expense or to the advantage of the dollar is an open question. The answer will depend in no small measure on whether the international financial markets have the kind of confidence in a future European Central Bank that, for example, the Deutsche Bundesbank has earned at home and in the international financial markets in the course of many years of a confidence-building monetary policy.

Although expectations regarding not only interest-rate movements but also political developments play a role in the competition among reserve currencies, domestic price stability is the most important factor for a reserve currency—in the long run at any rate. Provided that the United States succeeds in reestablishing and maintaining domestic price stability so that dollar assets continue to be a store of value, the dollar has every chance of remaining the principal reserve currency. Conversely, the future European currency will be all the more likely to take the place of the deutsche mark and gain importance as a reserve and investment currency, also vis-à-vis the dollar, the sooner the markets are convinced that the monetary policy of the European System of Central Banks is successfully geared to domestic price stability.

If that did occur—and I hope that a future European Central Bank will see this as its first duty—the role of the dollar in international transactions, and hence also as a reserve currency, may be reduced in relative terms by the emergence of a European currency as a major world currency. In all probability this will be a gradual development, and its impact on the U.S. economy is likely to be minimal.

One consequence of integrating the European economies into a large single market, and its culmination in a monetary union, will be a substantial contraction of the foreign trade sector. The share of foreign trade and capital transactions in the Community's combined gross national product and financial markets will be considerably smaller than the proportion, sometimes extremely high, in individual member economies. At present, total exports to third countries account for about 10 percent of the Community's aggregate GDP, a figure roughly equal to the corresponding U.S. ratio.

Therefore, fluctuations in the exchange rate will have a smaller impact than hitherto on the Community's real economy. These effects have already been significantly reduced since the creation of the exchange-rate mechanism and the gradual stabilization of exchange-rate relationships within the European Monetary System. Even under the recently more stable intra-European exchange-rate conditions, however, the various EC currencies have still been affected to differing degrees by shifts out of or into the dollar (of which the deutsche mark was usually the main counterpart), and these shifts have been a constraint on the individual member countries' monetary and interest-rate policies. Such pressures on internal monetary cohesion will disappear once the European Community has irrevocably fixed intra-Community exchange rates and established a single currency and once, as a logical consequence, it pursues a common monetary policy. And though major dollar fluctuations will continue to influence the overall situation in the Community, any immediate adverse effects will become more tolerable than under present conditions.

These comments should not be seen as a plea for a policy of "benign neglect" for the exchange rate. But, as has been demonstrated by the United States with its repeated pursuit of a policy of benign neglect in the past, a large domestic market is able—at least to some degree and for a certain period of time—to absorb the impact of exchange-rate movements better than economies with large foreign trade sectors. International cooperation will nevertheless remain necessary, but it could be based less on the goal of keeping exchange rates stable and more on the primary goal of keeping prices stable. If the world's leading economies succeed in achieving and maintaining domestic price stability, they will at the same time make a strong contribution to exchange-rate stability. The remarkable stability of exchange rates in the European Monetary System for a number of years now is, after all, the result of such price-stability-oriented economic, fiscal, and monetary policies in the member countries.

The statutes of the future common monetary authority of the European Community include a strong commitment to price stability as its primary objective. By pursuing such a policy at the Community level, monetary authorities in an economically unified Europe will be less likely to be confronted with the well-known dilemma of domestic versus exchange-rate stability that has often been faced even by the larger member economies. This does not necessarily mean that the European Community will become a hesitant participant in international monetary cooperation. The scope for influencing exchange rates through intervention in the foreign exchange markets may become even larger, since the impact on the liquidity of the banking system and the financial markets in general, resulting from those interventions, will be relatively smaller in a large currency area than it was in smaller member economies. But even close cooperation will not always rule out the possibility that an attempt to stabilize exchange rates through intervention and interest-rate policy could impair the conduct of a monetary policy geared to domestic stability.

There will therefore still be a need for some elasticity in exchange rates between such currency areas as the United States and a future united Europe, to allow for differences in inflation performances and interest-rate movements. But because of their similar size, the dollar area and the European monetary union will be better able than smaller economies to absorb the impact of exchange-rate movements on their real economies and to cope with such movements.

CONCLUSION

From time to time, not least in the United States, concerns are voiced that a European monetary union will take the Community further down the road to a "Fortress Europe." I am confident that such concerns will prove unfounded. In the financial area we have over the last few years seen a steady strengthening of those forces within the Community that insist on capital liberalization for all countries rather than between member countries only. We have seen the adoption of the principle of national treatment—with foreign financial institutions operating through branches or affiliates in the EC treated in the same way as domestic institutions—sensibly applied, rather than crude reciprocity, as the basis for the banking and securities trading regimes of the Community. Furthermore, in their design of a future European System of Central Banks, the governors of the EC central banks have been inspired by liberal views of the functioning of modern-day economies. The statute of the European System of Central Banks states that "the System shall act consistently with free and competitive markets." This is intended to ensure that the European System of Central Banks will pursue its monetary policy functions without recourse to methods and instruments that would interfere with market processes, such as direct quantitative or other credit restrictions and interest-rate ceilings.

Generally speaking, European integration will bring more opportunities than perils for the United States. American business has already benefited from the tearing down of internal EC barriers as part of the Community's single-market program. The U.S. economy will benefit from a strong, anti-inflationary performance by one of its major trading partners. If the European monetary union contributes, as is intended, to creating a stable and growth-oriented economy in Europe that remains open to international trade, its benefits will not be limited to Europe but will also be felt in the United States and throughout the world.

Kurt Biedenkopf

7

A Reunified Germany and the Unification of Europe

G ERMAN UNIFICATION was at the same time European unification, and the elimination of the division of Germany was at the same time the elimination of the division of Europe. When the coup in the Soviet Union failed in August 1991, someone said, in my opinion correctly, that Russia had returned to Europe. Europe suddenly expanded farther into the east than before the attempted coup. It was indeed impressive to witness Mikhail Gorbachev and Boris Yeltsin seal and give final testimony to this process in an American television broadcast. These two leaders told the world that communism had been a tragic failure and that it should never happen again. This was a lesson, Gorbachev said, that all people must learn.

The consequences of this dramatic development, of course, involve not only the eastern part of Germany but all of Europe. These new circumstances substantially affect the European equilibrium established while Europe was divided, European

security policy and its objectives, and the international responsibilities of both Germany and the European Community. The
latter, thanks to its own dynamism, is now preparing the ground
for the creation of a unified currency and a new stability in
Europe. The European Community within its own framework
aided the reunification of Germany, and by integrating it into
Europe, helped to overcome the fears that a united Germany
would otherwise have aroused among its western and eastern
neighbors.

As for German reunification, one can witness under almost
laboratory conditions the effects of an attempt to change a
command economy into a market economy and the tasks that
arise when forty or fifty years of totalitarian structures and
their social, cultural, political, and educational consequences
must be overcome. I list those consequences because Western
nations sometimes focus too closely on the economic aspect
of integration and do not take into account that an economy
is also a cultural institution, that the development of economies
is largely determined by a society's level of education, by its
cultural standing, by its traditions and values, and by the social
structures of the society in which the economy operates. The
West is discovering from the experience of eastern Germany
how important these prerequisites for a market economy are,
issues not usually considered in studying the economic systems
of Western Europe, the United States, or Japan.

LESSONS OF GERMAN REUNIFICATION

The legal system is an indispensable prerequisite for a market
economy. And the destruction of the legal system as it is known
in Western culture is one of the most severe and lasting dam-
ages that communism inflicted in East Germany and in all
other areas where it had the opportunity to govern. The de-

struction of the legal system means that for many years these countries have had no experience with a private law society, no experience with organizing human relations through private law, through contract, cooperation, competitive processes, and property. The knowledge of how to live and work in a private law society is minimal in the generations that grew up in East Germany after the Second World War, though it is considerably more advanced and developed than in the Soviet Union or in some of the other Eastern European countries.

Even under the ideal conditions of reunification in Germany, however, it is difficult to extend the legal system on which a market economy and democracy rest to the eastern part of Germany. First one must find judges who can apply the effective legal regime and lawyers who can facilitate contractual arrangements as well as the founding of corporations; then one must convince the population that it can trust the law. Citizens must realize that all state and governmental activities are subject to due process. Without trust in the law, it is almost impossible to operate a market economy. Every citizen needs to be able to trust the law to protect his autonomy, his property, and the contracts he enters into. The West must keep this in mind as it tries to bring a market economy to Eastern Europe.

Doing so will be one of the main tasks to be resolved. I therefore believe the first lesson that can be learned from German integration is that the willingness to assist in the reconstruction process cannot be made dependent on the existence of a market economy. On the contrary, the *objective* of assistance and cooperation should be the willingness to assist in the creation and long-range development of a free economy determined by markets.

The second important problem that now confronts us and that is, I believe, common to the reform of command economies is the almost total depletion of all financial reserves. The socialist government in East Germany was capable of raising the

economy to the level of the early 1970s in West Germany and
Western Europe, but no further. A command society seems
incapable of increasing society's complexity beyond a certain
level. If it wants to increase its economic activities further, it
must deplete all available resources. That has happened. The
capital reserves and the ecology of eastern Germany are de-
pleted, and the population has been exploited. So aside from
having to build new functioning enterprises—small, medium,
and large entities of economic activity—we must correct the
depletion, rebuild capital reserves, overcome the tremendous
ecological damage, and restore the level of professional qualification among the population.

The level of professional qualification in eastern Germany
is approximately the same as that of France and West Germany
twenty years ago. But this problem is manageable. The population has a long tradition of achievement, especially in the
Free State of Saxony, that can now be continued without the
restrictions of a planned economy. The same is true in northern
Bohemia, Czechoslovakia, and other areas with a long history
of industrial activity. What is now the Free State of Saxony
was, after the First World War, the region with the highest
productivity per capita in all Germany. The situation in Bohemia was similar. It produced some of the finest machinery and
automobiles, had a highly developed textile industry, and created some interesting interdependencies both between industry
and the universities and between industry and cultural life.

Nevertheless, the damage is enormous. Germany is investing
billions of marks a year to requalify and retrain workers and
to help them overcome unemployment. The change from a
command society to a market economy is necessarily accompanied by very high unemployment. It means an almost total
reallocation of human resources, since a main goal of the socialist economy was total employment of the population. In
the former East Germany, the rate of employment in relationship to the employable population was 92 percent; the partic-

ipation rate in western Germany is 65 percent. This rate is an expression of high labor productivity and the efficient organization of the use of labor resources in an advanced economy. The high rate of employment in socialist economies is therefore not only the result of an ideological goal—namely, to include as many workers as possible—but also the expression of very low labor productivity.

I once thought that the distribution of wealth would become easier as a society became richer. I am beginning to learn that the opposite is true. The wealthier a society is, it seems, the more difficult it is to share, because everything, including the growth rate, has already been distributed. And it seems to be politically difficult to integrate large transfer payments into existing structures of income distribution. Nevertheless, we must manage, and we will manage.

I mention this difficulty not only because of the transfer payment problem as such but because German unification will change not only the five new federal states but all of Germany. The inclusion of five new Länder in the political structure of Germany is already a substantial change. The old coalitions that have been established in western Germany among the Länder and among the political parties are disturbed, to say the least. New coalitions are forming, which should be an advantage for all of Germany as well as for eastern Germany. The federal structure in Germany is growing stronger because the Länder will have to bear a large part of the responsibility for integration, especially in such areas as culture, education, and research where real wealth and the future are determined. We will also have to negotiate a new structure of horizontal and vertical income distribution among the various levels of government within the framework of our constitution. Since this system of distribution is of fundamental importance to a federal system, we are, in fact, renegotiating our federal system by renegotiating the distribution of income.

The motivation of the population is probably the most important prerequisite for a rapid and successful completion of the process. This, however, means that the contribution of the population in the areas involved must be recognized. Eastern Germans cannot make financial contributions, but they can make very substantial individual and political contributions to the process. In assessing and weighing the burden sharing within Germany as a whole, the noneconomic and nonfinancial contributions must be accepted as being as important as the economic and financial contributions. We hope they will be; at least we will talk about them until they are.

A positive consequence of German integration is the opportunity for modernization, especially in the public sector. We in eastern Germany are attempting to restructure our public sector in many ways that West Germany, for historical reasons and because of the influence of vested interests that developed in the last thirty years, did not choose to employ. One important aspect is the participation of private corporations and capital in developing the public infrastructure. In my state, we would like to see the water supply, sewage, and garbage disposal systems and other parts of the infrastructure privately planned, built, financed, and operated.

So much for the German process. Our main objective is to place the process of restructuring the East German economy into a larger framework. For that purpose, we have suggested that the revitalization of the three industrial regions of Saxony, northern Bohemia, and Upper Silesia should be considered a common European task, undertaken in the context of a Euroregion. In this Euroregion we would like to establish a network of regional cooperation even before Czechoslovakia and Poland become associated to or become members of the European Community. This cooperation should not center around the solution of ecological and transportation problems, but, to the extent possible, it should include a parallel development of industrial activities. This requires a careful consideration of the lessons learned during German unification as regards the sequence of economic integration and convertibility of currency.

At the beginning of German unification, most economists believed that, first of all, the economy would have to be rebuilt as a prerequisite for convertibility; then, as the crowning closure of this process a common currency would be introduced. In Germany, we learned that this sequence does not work. People simply said: "If the deutsche mark does not come to us, we will go to the deutsche mark." They were unwilling to wait until their own economies were strong enough for convertibility to be introduced. Western leaders are discussing at present—I have not yet formed an opinion on it—to what extent this experience applies to other central and eastern European countries, including the Soviet Union. Is it possible to reconstruct economies in a former socialist command economy without some semblance of convertibility? Is it possible to create the kind of international trade and exchange of labor essential for the development of these economies without some form of convertibility as a common economic denominator? I have discussed this issue with World Bank and International Monetary Fund officials, who, I felt, were somewhat doubtful whether the project of industrialization and redevelopment could succeed without some form of convertibility.

CHALLENGES FOR WESTERN EUROPE AND THE UNITED STATES

As regards the West, two facts need to be emphasized. First, with the end of the division of Europe, which, as noted, coincides with the end of the division of Germany, the old bipolar structure in Europe has disappeared. The security systems that were formed during the last forty years were built on the bipolar structure and managed the level of complexity connected with that structure. Now in a changed situation, the multiplicity of European regions, nationalities, and nations is being revitalized. Although until the Berlin Wall came down the basic objective of security policy was to maintain the status quo in Europe and to protect Western Europe from aggression from the East, now most dangers to Western security come from the inability to control the changes taking place in Eastern Europe. Managing the breakdown of a colonial system—the Stalinistic system amounted to that—is extremely difficult and requires being able to handle complexity on a much higher level than before. It will be very important to consider how these changes will affect the Atlantic community and NATO, as well as the European Community and other bodies of international cooperation.

Because of the uncertainties surrounding the outcome of the second Russian revolution and the possible instability of Eastern Europe, the American military presence in Europe remains an important security guarantee. No doubt the changed circumstances will permit a reduction of American troop strength on the Continent, but the continued presence of certain American and Canadian units would nevertheless be useful because they tie Europe's security to that of North America's. Even if Europe acquires greater capacities in its foreign and defense policies, NATO will retain a very special function; it would therefore be a mistake to allow that function to wither away. One day NATO may become superfluous, but in the uncertain climate of the 1990s this is improbable. That is why, in such turbulent times, it is a mistake to worry about the architecture of Europe's security. The aim should be to improve Europe's own defense capabilities without undermining the American security guarantee. Any dispute over the different functions of NATO and the Conference on Security and Cooperation in Europe is unnecessary because the latter does not offer the kind of security guarantee NATO represents for the democracies of Western Europe.

Second, the opening of Eastern Europe, and the need to provide at least a partial revitalization of its industrial structures, means that the West will have to open its markets to Eastern European developments. Highest priority must be given to helping the Eastern European republics—former Soviet republics or independent states—to regain their ability to feed their own people. In other words, great efforts must be made to reduce the waste that now exists in the Soviet Union, especially in transporting the harvest from the farm to the consumer. A recent Harvard University study showed that between 30 and 40 percent of all produce is spoiled before it reaches the consumer. Western nations must also help to increase the productivity of the farm structures, so that the Soviet Union need no longer spend hard currency reserves to feed its population. Rather, these reserves must be made available to increase industrial productivity and transform the gigantic military production complex.

If that is accomplished, the consequences for Europe and America will be considerable. For example, if Western countries do what they must do—namely, teach the people in the former Soviet Union how to feed themselves—that will have immediate repercussions on the farmers in the United States who have been exporting large amounts of grain to the Soviet Union and have accordingly expanded their production to service that need. This production will have to be diverted or discontinued.

But even closer to home, if Ukraine is learning to produce with Western methods, Ukraine will again become the breadbasket of Europe. That will have serious repercussions on the farm policy of the European Community, especially in France but also in Germany and to a certain extent in Great Britain. Many people are not yet aware to what extent the revitalization of Eastern Europe will require readjusting the economic structures inherited from a divided Europe. Including the Eastern European economies in the unified Europe will mean dispensing with certain productions in Western Europe that developed as a result of the division. That will probably be the most difficult problem to overcome because it affects vested economic and political interests in Europe as well as in the United States.

Other likely restructuring processes will occur in Western Europe and, to a certain extent, in the United States. One of the most important contributions to future security in Europe will be the willingness of Western Europe and the United States to subject themselves to such an open-market policy, allowing at least a degree of industrialization on a competitive basis in the eastern and southeastern parts of Europe. I will not elaborate here on the many difficult details of this situation.

As a sample of the problem, an eastern German coal miner recently asked me how he and two-thirds of his colleagues could be dismissed from their jobs with a settlement payment of not more than 4,000 marks, while the federal government supports jobs in the coal mining industry in western Germany at a rate of 70,000 marks per job per year. It is of course impossible to answer that question. The only response can be that this situation has indeed developed, but that now it is important to cope with change. I am speaking about an area in which change immediately meets the most strongly organized resistance from vested interests. But experience with all interest groups shows they are much alike in their ability to master political resistance against change. In my opinion, a primary challenge that Europe, and Western Europe in particular, faces is the need to adapt to the changes brought about by the reopening of Europe toward the East.

The alternatives that face the countries of Western Europe are either to engage actively in overcoming the tremendous difficulties in the east and southeast of Europe by ingenuity, manpower, supply of know-how, and of course funds, or to wall themselves in to protect themselves from mass migration from east to west. The political and economic costs of the second alternative are probably much higher—at least in the medium or long run—than the costs of going to the source of the problem and trying to remedy it. And that is true not only for Eastern Europe but also for the Mediterranean countries, especially those on the coast of North Africa.

So even as the West reflects with great joy on having overcome the bipolar structures of the Cold War, it must also realize that it has inherited new challenges. The old saying goes that the solved problem is the father of a new one. And Western leaders are now defining this new problem by attempting to chart Europe's, particularly the European Community's, political course for the years to come.

Giovanni Agnelli

8

An Industrialist's Answer
to Where Europe Is Going

A FTER THE MOMENTOUS POLITICAL CHANGES that have taken place in the former communist bloc over the last few years, prospects for the partnership between the United States and Europe present new opportunities and challenges. These underlie the creation of a new world order, where international cooperation may be improved and "regional" disputes handled to the greatest advantage of the parties involved, environmental issues tackled most profitably, raw materials and other resources properly allocated, and developing countries provided with appropriate financing. It seems that President George Bush had these and other issues in mind when on several occasions he laid emphasis on the importance of the Euro-American partnership, indicating that together we represent the basis of the "commonwealth of freedom" around which the other nations of the world are congregating.

Europeans and Americans may ask themselves why transatlantic partnership remains so important after nearly fifty years; a partnership that makes us by no means a negligible part of the world, occupying as we do 21 percent of the land-mass, with 11 percent of the world population, 48 percent of global output, and 60 percent of automobile production. The answer is that it is a partnership made up of deeply rooted relations and shared experience in all sectors of activity—pol-itics, security, economics, science, and culture. As Dennis Bark has commented, "If there is any example in today's world where common heritage and common interests are reflected in common values, it is the friendship and alliance of the Euro-peans and the Americans."[1]

Although our relationship has traditionally developed in terms of bilateral relations between the United States of Amer-ica and the single countries of Western Europe, today we notice a parallel development in bilateral links between the United States and the European Community. The joint statements now regularly issued at the end of EC-U.S. half-yearly consultation meetings clearly imply this development.

The impetus given to EC-U.S. relations underlines their growing importance in the eyes of both parties, particularly those of the European Community. Why is that? It is a result of Western Europe's new course, a course that in years to come will profoundly affect the old continent as well as the Euro-American partnership.

THE NEW DIRECTION OF EUROPE

First of all, we should ask ourselves where Western Europe is heading. This question received a strong answer during the Heads of State and Government summit in Maastricht in De-cember 1991. The outcome of the summit is that, on a conti-nental scale, Western Europe has now been provided with the means for irreversibly integrating and harmonizing, to an extent never before achieved in modern times.[2] The European Community has thus established its road map into the twenty-first century.[3]

This road map sets the following milestones: (1) completion of the single market by December 31, 1992, when it takes the place of the twelve separate domestic markets; (2) pursuit of a parallel plan intended to establish economic and monetary union, its foremost goal being a single currency by the end of the 1990s; (3) attainment of ever-closer political union, designed to work out common security and defense policies; and (4) investment of the Community with the power to elaborate policies aimed at strengthening bonds inside as well as outside its borders.

These milestones honor the commitment and efforts of politicians from member states. In my opinion, however, there is another objective that should be added to those just mentioned: establishment of an efficient industrial policy to ensure that European industry operates in the environment it needs to flex its muscles in view of the new competitive challenges it must face.

Clearly enough, in an age of increasing economic interdependence, it is the duty of European companies to withstand the challenge from their competitors on international markets. And while companies need Europe, Europe cannot stand without an industry structure of its own if it wishes its present prosperity to be maintained in the face of increasing social demands.

Enlarging the Community

Another challenging issue is whether the Community should be widened to include new members, and if so, to what extent. Several countries have asked to become members. This prospect should be debated in depth, and before fostering it, it seems appropriate to ensure that the Community's policy of integration, as set out in Maastricht, is significantly implemented. And when it is decided to bring in new members, it seems wise to let in first those countries whose political and economic systems are nearest to our own.

It is clear that East Germany's unification with West Germany, which has further strengthened the country's economic and demographic role within the Community, is also the first step in the extension of the European Community. However, this event was one Germans had been expecting for decades. Furthermore, it was undeniably right, and politically and historically unavoidable once the Iron Curtain and the Berlin Wall had collapsed following the momentous transformations in the former Soviet Union and popular uprisings in eastern and central Europe.

Assisting Eastern Europe

Helping those countries through their political and economic transition is a great challenge to the whole industrialized world. Well-coordinated political and financial cooperation on our part is without doubt indispensable from this viewpoint. And companies, too, can play a role of no little importance. This is true despite the many political uncertainties in Eastern Europe, the likelihood that the transition will be protracted, and the effect of all that on corporate investment strategies.

What can Western companies do, then? They can start to explore the area with attention and an attitude of understanding, flexibility, and willingness to cooperate. Under these terms, Western enterprises can act as a conveyor belt for market economy and entrepreneurial values in an area that has either forgotten what these values stood for or has never even encountered them before.

Because of the capacities of these populations, the international industrial group that I chair continues to believe in their growing markets and to invest in them in line with a strategic decision taken some time ago. Our business relations with these countries span many decades, and in most instances they began well before World War II. We therefore believe we have the experience necessary to overcome the inevitable stumbling blocks underlying the transition process now under way.

Political Integration

There can be no doubt that the European Community as a whole will work better with Eastern European countries the more it develops into an experienced player on the international scene and a player with a single voice. It is a well-known fact that all reference to a European federation was avoided in the Maastricht decisions. The process of political integration thus set in motion is nevertheless likely to proceed in a federal direction.

What is taking place in Western Europe is a highly important example of regional economic aggregation. It is a phenomenon occurring elsewhere, too, but in Europe it is unique because of the nature and complexity of the goals pursued and the number of participants involved. All this explains the different visions that often create a lack of unanimity in decision-making.

What we are likely to see in the near future is a merger of states, in which the whole has a distinct importance of its own with respect to the parts, thus producing a greater degree of unity but, at the same time, safeguarding the member states' individual cultural and domestic traits. It is interesting to notice that a similar federal model for Europe was envisaged by Victor Hugo as early as 1848, in a period when the leading European countries were often fiercely opposed to one another.[4] We may therefore conclude that, in time, the efforts of the Twelve will produce an economic and political union strongly resembling that achieved more than two centuries ago by the United States (the time required will depend on how much sovereignty the single member states are willing to forgo).

How does the United States fit into this process? In my opinion the United States, owing to its federal traditions, is in a perfect position to appreciate both the political and the economic aspects of European Community integration. The American attitude expressed in this regard shows a degree of understanding similar to that of the American multinationals. What is more, the United States itself has thought it appropriate to pursue a similar "regionalization" venture known as the North American Free Trade Agreement, encompassing Canada and Mexico, and is assessing comparable projects with the countries of the Pacific Rim.

RELATIONS WITH THE UNITED STATES

So what should we say, then, to those who still have reservations about Western Europe's intentions? Well, I wish to point out that, faced as Europe is by the increasingly inadequate decisionmaking potential of individual states in response to surging social, political, and economic demands, the transformation of the European Community is the only pragmatic, feasible answer in our age of unprecedented globalization.

And once this new Europe is born, it will not stand alone. My view is that this venture will by no means be a protectionist venture or, in other words, a Fortress Europe.[5] On the contrary, Europe will move in such a way that its interests are reconciled with those of the rest of the world. The degree of openness of our venture, which is both a specific trait of the Community and one of its main principles, emerges clearly from the U.S.-EC trade statistics. These data show the following:

—the U.S. trade deficit with the EC, amounting to U.S. $13 billion in 1984, declined to $1 billion in 1989, then disappeared; in 1990 there was a trade surplus of U.S. $3 billion;

—the EC is the most attractive foreign market for the United States, receiving as it does about 20 percent of U.S. merchandise exports;

—sales of U.S. multinationals in Europe amount to six times U.S. exports to the EC; and

—U.S. investments in Europe during the last three decades reached a total of 126 billion European currency units.

Continuation of the integration process should be regarded simply as a step that the Community has to take for the sake of consistency; and only by acting accordingly will it be able to offer the United States further opportunities for cooperation.

A Permanent GATT Institution

I do not, however, wish to depict transatlantic partnership more optimistically than is realistic. Not everything is plain sailing between the United States and Europe, and problems and contrasts do occasionally arise. But what is important is how partners seek to solve their disputes. In this respect, the way the Community and the United States began to tackle their disagreement in 1991 over agricultural subsidies is a good sign if we consider that it was—and remains—perhaps one of the worst disputes to date.

The disagreement was all the more noteworthy because at the end of 1990 it brought to a stalemate four years of the Uruguay Round of GATT negotiations among more than one hundred countries. Many participants actually accused the European Community of jeopardizing the future of the multilateral trade systems in the fifteen fundamental areas considered in the negotiations, which include intellectual property and services and investments.

For several reasons, European industry lays a great deal of importance on the successful conclusion of these negotiations. First, a well-functioning, widespread multilateral trade system thwarts any temptation to exchange it for either bilateral trade agreements or trade blocs. Second, the system will ensure a goal that has always been supported by the GATT: continued expansion in worldwide trade. Figures show, in fact, that trade grew from U.S. $70 billion in 1960 to U.S. $3 trillion in 1989, with a 50 percent increase over the last eight years. Third, the GATT system may thus improve the prospects of developing countries, and primarily those of eastern and central European countries, new players in the market economy and worldwide trade.

All these goals can be achieved if one very clear condition is met: improvement of GATT functioning and rules, which are virtually unchanged since the GATT was established, despite its founders' insight, and which are proving increasingly inadequate to perform its many important tasks.

Security and Defense

If the economic prospects for the U.S.-EC partnership appear good, so do those regarding security and defense. The role of NATO—which proved fundamental even outside the European continent during the Gulf war—was solemnly confirmed in Rome in October 1991. Although the military and political "threat" that it was established to counter more than forty years ago has lessened, NATO, adequately restructured, will remain a bulwark in the new environment. The newly established North Atlantic Cooperation Council is a first step in this direction. The council will cooperate with the Conference on Security and Cooperation in Europe in tackling the surging conflicts and ethnic strife in Eastern Europe and the former Soviet Union.

CONCLUSION

We cannot deny that there have been ups and downs in the relations between the United States and the western part of the European continent. I do believe, however, that the soundness of our partnership is unquestionable and that it will improve further, provided that we are able to profit from future opportunities as we have done in the past.

To return to Victor Hugo's ideas about Europe in 1848, here is how he imagined our impending relations: "The time will come when these two immense systems—the United States of America *and the United States of Europe*—will come face to face with one another, shake hands and trade their products, their arts, their genius . . . thus improving the state of our world."[6] As we move beyond the 500th anniversary of Europe's discovery of the New World, there is no reason why Hugo's prophecy—that meanwhile has already become a reality—should not continue to apply in the future.

NOTES

1. Dennis L. Bark, "America's Heritage?" in A. Anderson and Dennis L. Bark, eds., *Thinking about America in the 1990s* (Stanford University, Hoover Institution, 1988), p. 124.

2. This process of integration, which has been under way for over forty years, began in the early 1950s with the establishment of the European Coal and Steel Community; it slowed down during the 1970s, but started up again with renewed determination and ambition during the mid-1980s.

3. The Maastricht decisions are included in a treaty signed in February 1992, which still needs to be ratified by the parliaments of the individual member states of the Community.

4. A European federalist doctrine saw its prime in 1848, in 1866–67, and again during World War I; it gave rise to a political party organization during World War II.

5. This is a commitment that many failed to appreciate for a long time and that some people still believe.

6. Translated from Victor Hugo, "*Discours inaugural du Congrès de la Paix*," in *Oeuvres complètes: Actes et paroles* (Paris: Metzel, 1882).

James Schlesinger

9

An American Assessment: "Hands across the Sea" Less Firmly Clasped

G IVEN THE STIRRING DRAMA of the changes in the East and the lesser (though still impressive) drama of steps toward greater European unity, the issue of prospective U.S.-European relations has understandably been overshadowed. Indeed, to the extent that it has been addressed at all, it has been almost as an afterthought. Yet such massive changes in the structure of international politics must inevitably bring major adjustments, some of which will be unforeseen. Not only will it take many years for such adjustments to take place, but it may also take years before they are broadly acknowledged. Such is likely to be true for U.S.-European relations in the aftermath of the Cold War.

It is particularly likely to be the case on this side of the Atlantic, for the collapse of the Warsaw Pact, the withdrawal of Soviet forces from Eastern Europe, the end of the Soviet threat, and, indeed, the disintegration of the Soviet Union must ultimately mean a lessened role and lessened influence for the

United States in Europe. Americans will be inclined to remi-
nisce about the glory of Cold War days and consequently will
be slow to acknowledge America's diminished role and status.
Europeans, understandably delighted by the end of the division
of Europe and of the residue of World War II, will be far more
inclined to recognize these changes in the role of the United
States, but for reasons of gratitude, diplomacy, or tactics, they
will be disinclined to stress so fundamental a change in the
relationship to their American brethren. However, time and the
unfolding of events will make that change increasingly evident
to the discerning.

For the moment, however, the catharsis reflecting the Western (largely American) triumph in the Cold War—along with
the preponderant American role in the Gulf War—has tended,
at least temporarily, to obscure the immense changes already
in train. Nonetheless, in examining the prospects for U.S.-
European relations, one should at the outset acknowledge two
fundamental facts. First, ultimately the realities of the changed
political and economic lines of forces will outweigh all the
immediate declamations of unswerving mutual loyalty, or of
fidelity to institutions (like NATO), which shall remain undiminished despite the change in mission. Second, the sharply
diminished need for U.S. protection unavoidably implies a
shrinkage in the U.S. importance to Europe. That will be true
no matter how much we flatter ourselves (and the Europeans
flatter us) regarding our being the "sole remaining superpower." A military superpower simply cannot deal with nu-
merous adjustments—almost all modest, if not Lilliputian, in
scope. A "superpower" is essential only for *major* military
tasks, such as deterrence. With the end of the Soviet threat
very few such tasks remain, and fewer still that Europeans
cannot handle on their own or for which the United States is
essential. For some of those tasks—providing massive economic aid to enable Eastern Europe to make the transition from

communism, for example—the United States has shown little appetite for participating in a substantial way.

Thus the outcome is easily predictable. U.S.-European relations, while remaining generally warm, will grow somewhat more distant and far less intimate. Increasingly the European nations will go about their business with less and less reference to the United States. The European movement toward "ever closer union" will continue apace, though far more gradually and with more setbacks than the enthusiasts will concede. But it will continue. The Americans will continue to offer advice, some solicited, some unsolicited, but increasingly that advice will be shrugged off. Indeed, even in the last three years, well before the completion of the withdrawal of Soviet forces from Eastern Europe, American advice has frequently fallen on deaf ears.

From time to time this newly manifested European independence has caused irritation and shock in Washington. The irritation is no doubt understandable; the sense of shock is not. It is scarcely surprising that Europeans regard developments in Eastern Europe, say, as matters that they are far more knowledgeable about and that are far closer to their interests. On such matters as the recognition of Slovenia and Croatia, they are likely to regard American advice as having a far-off, if not academic, sound. To be surprised by such attitudes reflects our own innocence and vanity.

To some extent the new European freedom to focus on distinct, as opposed to common, interests is desirable. It is one of the benefits of the virtual elimination of the common security threat. For forty-five years the main task of American foreign policy has been to allow the Western European states to flourish without interference from the East. Surely our success in achieving this long-time policy goal ought not make us too despondent.

Though to some degree this greater European independence

was unavoidable, to some degree it was not. The prospective distancing of the United States and Europe could have been mitigated if both sides had worked harder during the Cold War period to build common institutions. Take, for example, the famous (or infamous) ''year of Europe,'' which Secretary of State Henry Kissinger attempted to launch in 1973. No doubt the phrasing was unfortunate and the preparation was inadequate. But the purpose of the endeavor was grossly misunderstood in Europe. Kissinger's motive was a noble one, in part reflecting his position as an American of European birth. What he had hoped to do was to cement relations through institutions that would survive, when those American who had worked so long and closely with Europe and Europeans and had emotional ties were no longer on the scene.

Regrettably the effort proved abortive. The European nations were generally suspicious of American motives, rather unjustly so in view of Kissinger's high purpose. The timing was clearly unfortunate. Many in Europe had been distressed by the American involvement in Vietnam. Some, and a steadily growing number, were increasingly disturbed by the unfolding Watergate affair, which was to reach a crescendo in the following year. And, finally, the Western alliance was shortly torn by dissension during and after the Middle East war in the fall of 1973.

To have created institutional arrangements then would have established a more permanent bond between Europe and America. Unfortunately that was not to be. The opportunity, which the Cold War's sense of common purpose provided, was lost. Now, two decades later, it is no longer possible to forge so close a bond. We shall have to settle for a lesser solution. Warm relations will continue for the most part, but there will not be institutional arrangements that go beyond the North Atlantic Treaty Organization, designed primarily to provide military security rather than a permanent political bond.

"The Moving Finger . . . having writ, / Moves on." What will the future of U.S.-European relations be? I deal with this evolving relationship under the usual rubrics of security, economics, and politics.

SECURITY ARRANGEMENTS

For almost forty-five years security has been the crucial element in the U.S.-European relationship. Deterrence provided by the United States has been the essential glue holding the alliance together. Up to the end of World War II American leaders, including President Harry Truman, believed that the European states could work out their destinies on their own—and that after the war the United States could essentially "go home." But then the Soviet takeover of Eastern Europe, the communist danger within Italy and France, the coup in Czechoslovakia, the Berlin blockade, and, in 1950, the invasion of Korea destroyed this comforting illusion. To provide a counterweight to the Soviet power that threatened a divided and weakened Western Europe, the continued involvement of the American "superpower" would be required. American forces returned, in number, to Western Europe and have remained ever since. NATO was created and has served as the embodiment of mutual security. Europe lay under the protection of an ever more sophisticated U.S. nuclear deterrent. Europe's own contribution to the common defense began to grow. West Germany was embraced within the alliance, and German rearmament was launched. As Soviet capabilities increased, NATO doctrine was slowly adjusted. Flexible response, a robust conventional capability, and later the threat of selective nuclear strikes became integral to an increasingly sophisticated NATO deterrent. The feared Warsaw Pact assault never came.

Recent Changes

Now the security issue has been fundamentally altered. Contrary to all expectations, the external threat has largely evaporated. The Warsaw Pact has disappeared, and the residual Soviet threat has largely disintegrated. The need for massive security forces and complex security arrangements has correspondingly abated, weakening the glue that has held the alliance together. Consequently, the question has grown increasingly pressing: what is to succeed the security arrangements in providing the necessary glue—in particular, the glue that maintains American involvement in Europe? It seems fair to say that this fundamental question has not been addressed with any urgency. The clear tendency has been to rely on momentum, and to hope that the legacy of the past will be sufficient. Just as was true after World War II, it will probably take some years before an answer is sorted out.

The eruption of the Gulf crisis in August 1990—while the Soviet Union still appeared to possess unity and much of its global power and one year before the abortive coup attempt in Moscow— led briefly to a hope in President Bush's "new world order" as a continuing bond for members of the Western alliance. The phrase had a good wartime ring to it—and might sustain American engagement for the indefinite future. Perhaps to European ears it sounded a bit Wilsonian. Over the years Europeans have either become inured to or learned to be patient with these waves of American enthusiasm. (One recalls Clemenceau's weary reaction to Wilson's Fourteen Points: "Fourteen," he mused; "the Good Lord required only ten.") But the new world order faded quickly as a substitute for the security arrangements designed to cope with the classic Soviet threat. The Soviet Union, initially intended as one of the two superpower pillars of the new world order, soon collapsed. Moreover, the Bush administration itself quickly lost interest in and ceased to advertise the concept. Perhaps it had come to recognize the futility or the costs of coping with the chaos that marked the old Soviet empire, the Middle East, and much of the underdeveloped world. In any event, European skepticism about how orderly the post–Cold War world could be made to be was never put to the test.

NATO and its component military establishments were not slow to react. Indeed, by normal organizational or bureaucratic standards, they reacted with extraordinary rapidity, quickly recognizing that neither the Warsaw Pact nor the Soviet threat could any longer provide a foundation for NATO force planning or strategy. Consequently, they quickly recommended far smaller and more mobile forces, designed for crisis management, with a much reduced American component. They planned to construct a multinational Rapid Reaction Force, under the command of a British general, and intended to respond quickly to crises that could not be predicted in advance.

Whether this plan is the basis of a permanent substitute for the Soviet threat—and particularly one that can retain American involvement—remains to be seen. Quite clearly the first such crisis, the one in Yugoslavia, with the manifest American unwillingness to get directly involved and with the focus for a solution on the United Nations rather than on NATO, raised some question about the long-term adequacy of the suggested solution. In the end, it may wind up appealing only to the military establishment itself. Nonetheless, the military is to be commended for its quick recognition of the obsolescence of its time-honored force planning and doctrine, and for its imaginativeness in proposing a plausible change.

The U.S. Position

The United States was somewhat slower to change and somewhat less imaginative. The U.S. Department of Defense tended to cling to the threat from the East—up to the point of its evaporation. Here we were alone among our allies, who far more quickly recognized that the threat had largely disappeared. (In this regard things are not so much different from the past, for the European allies habitually took the Warsaw Pact threat far less seriously than the Americans did.) But surely even the residual historical threat becomes undermined, if not meaningless, when Russia itself asserts that it wants to join NATO.

We have also regularly claimed that the American presence and American leadership, as well as a vibrant NATO, will be required to cope with uncertainties and to prevent instability. Yet when the chaos and violence in Yugoslavia provided a first, rather dramatic example of such instability, Americans quickly declared that coping with the Yugoslav situation was up to the Europeans. The fact that I personally think that it was the correct policy does not vitiate the more impressive fact that this *political* decision undermined our own more general argument for the continued role of our forces in Europe.

The Defense Department hopes to maintain, after the drawdowns, a force of 150,000 troops in Europe. That force would include an Army corps in Germany. It remains to be seen whether Congress will be prepared to support so large a U.S. presence in Europe. But equally important, we have not yet determined whether the Europeans, and particularly the Germans, will be prepared to tolerate so large a force on their soil for the indefinite future, particularly after the completion of the Soviet troop withdrawal. The Kohl government is likely to be the most pro-American government we will ever see in Germany. But even that government has its own way of asserting its independence. To Washington's publicly expressed irritation, the Kohl government did not even answer the phone to take our frantic messages regarding the intended German recognition of Slovenia and Croatia. It seems to me most prudent not to set our aspirations for eternal friendship too high. Europe is likely to have its own and changing ideas about the size and composition of a residual American military deployment.

There is a significant risk that the United States will be seen to be clinging to the past. We have repeatedly insisted that the role of NATO will be transformed but not substantially reduced. We have been more or less open regarding the reason for our insistence on this large continuing role for NATO. It provides the only place for a continued American seat at the European table; it provides the only vehicle through which American leadership can be institutionally expressed. But surely we should recognize that the European view for such a role will be different from ours—and European enthusiasm, particularly in some nations, will be discernibly less. In brief, Americans continue to talk as if those important structural changes that we nominally acknowledge will have no real impact. The great mission for NATO is largely gone. While NATO will continue to have a significant political-military role, it will inevitably be one that is smaller than in the past. To pretend otherwise merely weakens U.S. credibility.

At the Rome summit in October 1991, President Bush urged our European allies that if they had doubts about the long-run American role in Europe and believed it to be ''superfluous,'' they should tell us now. To pose such a challenge in itself shows our own self-doubt about what our relationship to Europe should be. Moreover, it is unrealistic to expect the Europeans to declare *now* how they want the U.S. role in Europe to change. They do not know yet. Only time and the unfolding of events will determine and reveal what the Europeans collectively really want in the future relationship.

Finally, the United States has repeatedly expressed its apprehensions over European movement toward a more unified European military force. We have regularly expressed suspicion, no doubt excessive suspicion, about any serious moves toward Franco-German military integration. I believe this to be a mistake. In the first place, the degree of European military unity will be largely determined by internal dynamics, and will not, in any event, be much influenced by American expressions of concern. In the second place, we should bear in mind that for many years we have pressed the Europeans to achieve greater military cooperation. We should recall that four decades ago the United States strongly urged the establishment of the European Defense Community—and we were deeply disappointed when it was finally scuttled, under the Fourth Republic, by the French parliament. The Western European Union was then designed as a substitute for the EDC. If we then wanted the greater vehicle, we should not now object to the lesser vehicle. The WEU seems a highly appropriate vehicle for the pooling, to whatever extent the Europeans ultimately agree, of their military forces. It would be ironic if Americans now came to resent the achievement of their own long-term objective of greater European military integration. Admittedly the WEU may be a symbol that the United States has become less needed than it was during the Cold War. But if we wish to retain our influence in Europe and a continuing role in European security, we cannot afford to be churlish.

ECONOMIC CHANGE AND AMERICAN APPREHENSIONS

Just as concern about the common defense tends to be cohesive, so trade issues tend to be divisive. As worry over security diminishes, as the historic threat to Europe and to the West fades, attention increasingly shifts to economic issues. Such issues are less likely to unite the United States with, than to divide it from, the increasingly unified Common Market.

Examining how economic issues will affect the U.S.-European relationship requires assessing the impact of the single market, which will permit the free movement of trade and people. For the most part the movement toward a single market involves European decisions and European consequences that others are in a better position than I to discuss. All I can do is to offer an American view on this primarily European development. Suffice it to say that the United States has been far more concerned about the impact of "Europe 1992" and the single market than it has been about security or political issues. Americans have been highly ambivalent, at best, and apprehensive or hostile, at worst, about the effect of 1992. Much real fear has been expressed, most notably a fear of Fortress Europe. Many meetings have been held regarding the consequences of 1992, usually attended by those industries whose interests are either adversely or favorably affected. Such meetings may be a vehicle for reassurance, protest, or simply commiseration. In the end they are not likely to have much effect.

My view is that the attention devoted to and concern expressed about 1992 has been grossly disproportionate to its total effect on the United States, not to mention the degree to which Americans can influence decisions taken in Europe. No doubt the creation of a single European market could strongly affect specific industries—and that will require substantial adjustment. However, its overall impact on the American economy is likely to be modest. We should therefore not allow our apprehensions to get out of hand. Once again, it is important to bear in mind that for many years the United States has strongly encouraged the movement toward European economic integration. In this connection, as with security matters, it would not be fitting for us to appear churlish when the objectives for which we have long striven are finally achieved.

This is not to say that I think the impact of the single market will be inconsequential from the standpoint of specific Amer-

ican industries. Almost unavoidably the single market will be
a vehicle for joint discrimination against the United States. One
may accept European assurances that there is no desire or
intention to create a high-barrier Fortress Europe. That barriers
may be no higher in absolute terms does not mean they will
be no higher in relative terms. After all, the purpose of the
single market is to eliminate internal barriers, which inherently
means increased joint discrimination against the outside world.
Moreover, the process of negotiation and accommodation will
normally be at the expense of those who do not have to be
accommodated in that process.

For years Europeans have expressed their frustration at their
weakness relative to the United States and Japan in high-tech-
nology industries. Now that internal barriers are being re-
moved, it would be surprising if the opportunity to foster high
technology was not seized and that joint discrimination against
the outside world did not occur. To be sure, the United States
is likely to be far better treated than Japan. Nonetheless, the
higher *relative* barriers will encourage both nations to produce
in Europe.

The net effect will be to encourage international investment
and to discourage international trade. This certainly does not
imply that international trade will fail to grow, but it will grow
less than it would have otherwise. It will be discouraged by
the muting of the effects of price and cost differences but will
undoubtedly be encouraged by the growth of income.

The task for the United States in these circumstances is to
prevent the discrimination from getting out of hand, to discourage any increase in the absolute level of trade barriers, to
avoid getting too stirred up by the microeconomic horror stories
to which individual industries will point, and to avoid a general
trade war. We must retain a sense of proportion. Despite all
the chatter, the consequences for the United States of the move
to a single market are far less dramatic and far more favorable
than many in the political-military realm.

Moreover, changes will likely be far less immediate and far less extreme than advertised. Progress in practice will be slower than on paper. The expansion of the Common Market—to take in Austria and Sweden at an early date and others at a later date—will mean some sacrifice of the intensity of market integration.

Inevitably jealousies will continue to exist in Europe. There will be squabbles over the "cohesion fund." The poorer nations of southern Europe will argue that the fund is much too small and that they need much greater assistance. The richer nations of the North will be alarmed by and will probably resist the movement of industry toward the lower-wage South. Britain will prefer to move at a slower pace than the others and will have to be dragged along.

All the nations involved are democracies, sensitive to the concerns and interests of their own voters. They will be jumpy about any threat to older industries that causes a serious loss of jobs or income. Democracies are far better at creating, through direct or indirect subsidy, new industries (such as high tech) than they are in allowing older industries to decline without resistance.

The upshot is that Americans have less cause for apprehension than is frequently suggested. Far more alarm has been expressed than is justified. So long as no gross trade imbalance exists between the United States and Europe, the single market should not cause any changes with which we cannot live comfortably. No doubt adjustments will be required, but they will be no greater than a healthy American economy can readily accommodate.

On balance, therefore, we would be wiser to turn our attention elsewhere. If we are worried about the future of the American economy, the future of American competitiveness, and the future of American economic leadership, we would do better to attend to our own self-inflicted problems. The low rate of domestic saving, the modest level of domestic invest-

ment, the slow growth of productivity, particularly relative to
Germany and Japan, the budget deficit, the trade deficit, the
weaknesses of our system of primary and secondary education,
all these antedate Europe 1992. If we want to see economic
performance improve and if we want to move toward a resto-
ration of American economic leadership, we need to attend
first to our internal problems.

POLITICAL IMPLICATIONS

Since Marshall Plan days, some forty-five years ago, the United
States has more or less regularly supported the movement toward greater political unity in Europe. The U.S. public generally harbors few of the misgivings that have been expressed
about the effect on the United States of European economic
unity. To most Americans, who from time to time wonder what
all the quarrels in Europe have been about, a movement toward
a United States of Europe seems patently desirable. By and
large U.S. policy has regularly pressed in the same direction.
In the 1950s and 1960s the U.S. government was frustrated by
Britain's reluctance to cast its lot with Europe and consistently
prodded Britain in that direction. It was later appalled by
Charles de Gaulle's veto of British entry into the Common
Market. Indeed the United States has been more consistent in
its support of greater political unity in Europe than have several
of the major and minor European countries themselves.

On the other hand, there was always a minority of senior
officials and their advisers who, whatever lip service they might
render to European unity, questioned whether such a movement
was desirable from the American point of view. They felt that
the European states would gang up on the United States, would
decide among themselves on a common policy, and would
present the United States with a fait accompli, so that U.S.

influence and leadership would inevitably be weakened. From time to time this ambivalence, though not publicly expressed, was clearly evident. Yet real hostility to serious efforts toward European political unity was rare. By and large, most officials as well as the public have over the years been consistent supporters of the movement toward European political union.

Now that the movement seems to be heading toward fruition, there are apparently more second thoughts. Quite rightly the Maastricht summit in December 1991 made Americans ponder about the future of Europe and U.S.-European relations. But Maastricht also set off alarm among those who fear greater European political unity, a common economic policy, or the movement toward a common European defense that might diminish NATO.

In my view such fears are not worthy of this country. We are on the verge of achieving political objectives that the United States has supported for many years. Just as victory in the Cold War represented a triumph of American policy, so the movement toward greater unity represents a triumph not only of European policy but also of American policy. Maastricht lay down a blueprint: for a single currency, for a Central Bank, for a common foreign policy, and for a common social and economic policy. These are goals to be achieved within this decade, although Britain has publicly reserved its options.

Surely we should welcome these changes, though it is no longer an American task to urge the European states to proceed more rapidly than they themselves determine. Surely the United States has been frequently enough called on to intervene in Europe's civil wars to make us duly apprehensive about differences within Europe. The present movement reduces to an insignificant level the risk that Europe might once again engage in civil wars.

Nor should we expect squabbles to cease. The European ''nation'' is somewhat like the Arab nation in that its unity is far easier to conceptualize than to achieve. In practice, Europe is likely to conform to de Gaulle's vision of "Europe of the Fatherlands." Former prime minister Margaret Thatcher is but the latest of European leaders to resist the loss of national sovereignty. Such attitudes are not likely to disappear soon.

For the moment Britain is the center of resistance, expressing reservations that are felt, though unstated, elsewhere. John Major owes his position as prime minister to the "politics of Europe." Consequently, he has treated and will continue to treat the subject with care. While it may be desirable political tactics, it is not useful for the achievement of real political unity for Major to return to London after Maastricht and triumphantly declare, "game, set, and match to Britain."

Such tensions are not likely to go away for the foreseeable future. Differences among the major powers will be difficult to resolve. The economic tensions mentioned earlier will also be reflected in the political dimension—especially between the rich and the poor nations. Germany's neighbors are likely to view that country with trepidation as its relative power grows and as the process of absorbing the former East Germany is completed. In short, the process of unification will go on for decades. It is a process that Americans should support. From our standpoint it does not represent a clear and present danger.

In part, Americans tend to sympathize with the perplexities of their long-time British ally. The British dilemma is no doubt acute. But despite their hesitation, not to say recalcitrance, the British recognize that in the end they have no choice but to go along. This fact is well understood on the Continent. It was Jean Monnet, derisively referred to by de Gaulle as the "Father of Europe," who observed during similar circumstances in the late 1950s: "The British know a *fait accompli* when they see one . . . and once the Community is operating successfully, Britain will join."[1]

If Britain were to stand aloof, it would shrink its influence in the new Europe. A similar judgment seems appropriate regarding Britain's involvement in European defense. The reduced threat from the East means a lessened reliance on nuclear deterrence. But the substantial denuclearization of Europe's defense inevitably implies a smaller role for Britain. Under these new circumstances the conventional contribution will become more important; strategy and doctrine will change. Ultimately, the weight of Britain's contribution to the common defense and Britain's degree of influence will depend on its willingness to participate.

Europe's future problems will probably be less and less those of traditional military security. Demographic trends reveal quite starkly that the West in general, and Europe in particular, is shrinking relative to the outside world. Western Europe's problem will be that of burgeoning populations along its frontiers seeking to get in. Along the Mediterranean coast this means the Muslim peoples of the Maghreb, Egypt, the Levant, and Turkey. For Germany it is likely to mean a continued pressure for immigration from the states to the east, perhaps particularly from the former Soviet Union. Both from inside and from outside, the new Europe will face challenges aplenty.

CONCLUSION

As it turns out, the "year of Europe" will be 1992 rather than 1973. The "year" will be quite different from that which Henry Kissinger envisioned two decades ago. It will be almost all internally initiated, with little sponsorship from the outside; there will be no building of common institutions across the Atlantic. It will proceed further along the path to common policies and toward ever greater union, reflecting greater European self-confidence and greater maturity. It should be welcomed by Americans.

Because of the dominant role that the United States played during the Cold War years, many Americans will inevitably feel some nostalgia for those glory years. When an external threat diminishes, alliances grow less cohesive. Unavoidably, the old order changeth and adjustments must be made. The danger for Americans is that they will cling to the past. The danger for Europeans, given America's domestic travails, is that they will be too dismissive of the United States and therefore of the value of the U.S.-European partnership.

As for the United States, it needs to face up to its long-overlooked social and economic challenges. Unless we effectively grapple with our domestic ills, we will have neither the inclination nor the ability to lead. Indeed, our domestic performance will be far more important in determining our international role than either the single market or Maastricht. And both Europe and the United States must recognize that, despite the radical changes in the structure of international politics and in the U.S.-European relationship, the transatlantic partnership will have abiding value for the future.

NOTE

1. Quoted in George W. Ball, *The Past Has Another Pattern: Memoirs* (Norton, 1982), p. 209.

Henry Brandon

10

A More Promising Era
Beckons At Last

A T THE END OF THE CENTURY, indeed of a millennium, we are suddenly living in a time when history seems to have accelerated, and we are being swept forward at a reckless pace. It is for the reader of these pages to assess the rightness of judgments about our direction of travel or likely points of arrival. But when governments, nations, and institutions can hardly pause to take a breath to measure and weigh the consequences of headlong change, it is valuable that the contributors to this volume give us their views of what to expect from the future. It is significant, too, that from their diverse national and political viewpoints they are all inclined to assume that the European Community will gradually advance toward a single market and a single currency. But beyond that the predictions vary about the extent to which these changes will become springboards to a United States of Europe. Every week the European Community in Brussels makes minor decisions, invisible to the general public, to advance these objectives. And yet stability in the coming decade will in many ways depend on American-European relations, the basic theme of this book.

Successive American administrations have tended to encourage the idea of a federal Europe of some kind, including the administration of President George Bush. Of course, principle and practice can prove to be quite different. Both the president and some of his important senior officials are inclined to look askance, for instance, at how the European Commission is constituted; though responsible to hardly anybody, it can make decisions in the economic field directly affecting American interests, decisions that might well become too far advanced before the United States is able to bring any effective influence to bear. Some of the Commission's members are also said to be "aggressively unsympathetic," as one American dealing with them put it, which obviously will not contribute to American-European relations. As a result, the old enthusiasm has given way to ambivalent feelings about relations with the Community.

The contributors to this volume do not all interpret alike the consequences of the landmark Maastricht conference of December 1991 and the resultant treaty. Rocard views it as "pav[ing] the way toward an exacting, yet exciting, common future," while others point to the built-in uncertainties of its many political escape clauses. The differences reflect national positions: those taken by the Germans and the French, who favor an ever-closer union, and that preferred by the British, who wish to proceed at a more circumspect pace.

In my view, progress will be slower than envisaged at Maastricht. Since the twelve Community members set their calendar and wrote their catechism in December 1991, Europe has assumed a new political and geographical meaning. The European Community is not only moving toward accepting members of the European Free Trade Association (EFTA) such as Austria, Sweden, Finland, and Switzerland (which create institutional problems if not serious economic ones) but is also preparing "a coherent concept for the development of relations with Central, Eastern and South-Eastern Europe," as Chancellor Helmut Kohl said early in 1992.[1] In his mind Europe has become "all-Europe," which includes the successor states of the Soviet Union. Dangers on the way to a stable, peaceful Europe are not only the problems of economic reconstruction but also the reawakening of extreme nationalism, environmental hazards caused by unsafe Eastern European nuclear power plants, and the risks of nuclear weapons proliferation.

BRITAIN AND THE UNITED STATES

As regards the British, for a long time they either did not want to commit themselves to be part of Europe or did not believe the French and Germans would "bring off" the European Common Market, as Sir Evelyn Shuckburgh, head of the Western Department of the Foreign Office, put it.[2] Lord Thorneycroft, president of the Board of Trade, complained in 1955: "At the very moment when we ought to have been shaping the European Community, we were on the sidelines. ... We stood aside because there was no decision in the British Cabinet to play a part in Europe."[3] Jean Monnet once predicted that the British would make the fundamental change in their traditional policy toward Europe only after they saw that the new Community was operating—his prediction is more apt today than it ever was.

The fact that the British have now decided they must be part of the new Europe indicates the growing gravitational pull of the Community. The British know they will have to swallow hard to overcome their island psychology and their deep-seated attachment to century-old symbols of sovereignty as well as to face the devaluation of their "special relationship" with the United States. Volumes have been devoted to questions of the reality and the extent of this link, including its ebbs and flows. Without question, many important interests have been shared, but in some minds, mostly British, but by no means all, this relationship acquired a semimystical status. One high official at the British embassy in Washington once told me (and I had similar experiences with some of my London editors) that on occasion he had to make it clear to the Foreign Office in London, particularly when differences with the United States had occurred, that he was reporting from a foreign country. To recognize differences amounted almost to a culture shock, because of the assumption that if you said it in English, agreement was sure to follow.

On the other hand, although all British ambassadors arrived in Washington with high expectations about that mysterious blessing of the Anglo-American special relationship, as far as I can recall in my thirty-five years of reporting from the United States, all except two of them left disappointed about the inspirational effect it had and the influence it afforded them. The two exceptions were Sir Oliver Franks, because he served under the most pro-British secretary of state, Dean Acheson; and Sir David Ormsby-Gore, whose personal relationship with President John F. Kennedy was the zenith of his career.[4]

Discussing a European Community policy is therefore bound to have a different resonance in Washington than in London. However much the U.S. president might wish to improve his influence with the Community, the Anglo-American "special relationship" is not the recommended means. First, Washington would not want to be seen as trying to push the British into a less ambivalent posture toward the Community for U.S. purposes. Second, and more to the point, it would not want Britain to offer itself as, or seem to be, some kind of interlocutor between the United States and the Community. Other member states would be quick to resent such an assumption; America wishes to be free to play her own cards. It remains a delicate line to tread.

Bonds of language and culture are too strong for Britain to be suddenly treated by Americans as just another foreign country. While some links on matters of defense and intelligence are bound to decline in importance, some will nevertheless remain strong. Examples are the closely integrated signal link at Cheltenham, England, which goes back to World War II, and the kind of joint military operations, outside NATO, that was mounted in the Gulf War, when British officers were so integrated with the Americans that they were wearing American uniforms, and the two nationalities could be told apart, as General Sir Peter de la Billiere put it, only "by the length of their haircuts."[5]

THE SURVIVAL OF NATO

There has been much talk about whether NATO will be able to survive without the threat of the Soviet war machine. Actually, this question is more often raised in the U.S. Congress than in Europe—if we make due allowance for the French, who are too shrewd not to recognize the security offered by the United States and NATO, but who resent the United States for interfering with their ambition to be seen as the leading power in Europe, and NATO for providing the United States with a political as well as a military presence in Europe. Nevertheless, NATO's survival is not at risk. Not only do Western Europeans want to keep it on duty—they have little confidence in a Franco-German European force—but, paradoxical as it may seem, the Eastern Europeans are particularly anxious for NATO to play the European policeman. What they fear is the return of authoritarianism in the former Soviet Union.

In Washington in December 1991 President Vaclav Havel
of Czechoslovakia expressed in a private conversation his worries of calamities threatening from the East; namely, chaos in
the streets, disruptive waves of emigration to the West, risk of
local wars over many new and old contested frontiers, and the
proliferation of nuclear weapons. The newly created North
Atlantic Cooperation Council, whose members are former East-
West adversaries, not only will help to calm such worries about
instability but will give Eastern Europeans the psychological
comfort of a link to the most powerful nations in the West and
the hope that their indirect relationship to NATO, even if they
are not formally protected by a security guarantee, will affect
an aggressor's calculations. After all, much of foreign policy
is concerned with affecting calculations about whether the
game is worth the risks or the costs.

For the Czechs, the Poles, and the Hungarians, the continued
presence of a counter-Soviet military alliance borne of the Cold
War is an insurance against their disappearing through the
trapdoors of history. They are aware, better than many, of the
fragmentation inside the new Russian government and the military, and their continuing anti-Western feeling, and they are
urgently concerned that somehow, perhaps by means of aid,
the West will use its influence to help persuade the former
Soviet military to adhere to the accords controlling nuclear
weapons.

THE PROBLEM OF GERMANY

The British general Lord ("Pug") Ismay, according to friends
of his, once summed up NATO's mission in one brief sentence:
"NATO was invented to keep the Americans in, the Russians
out, and the Germans down." Most Europeans recognize that
a new democratic Germany has arisen impressively from the

ruins of Hitler's Reich, a Germany such as has never quite existed before. But however responsibly and cooperatively it behaves, the political weight and financial power it has already acquired have revived, if only at the back of many people's minds, the historically based fear that Germany (and now re-united Germany) might once again dominate Europe. For the 45 years of the Cold War there was no need to address the question, at least 120 years old, of how to absorb Germany in a nonthreatening way into a stable political system. But now the question must be faced anew.

What complicates American diplomatic efforts to seek the closest internal lines of influence in Bonn is the German desire, as a wit once put it, to have the Americans for a wife and the French for a mistress. The French see the European Community as an important anchor for Germany in the West, and the Germans see it as a symbol of their close relationship with the French. The Germans view their own membership of NATO as the basis for their Atlanticism and a European military force as the symbol of their Europeanism. Maneuvering between the two positions is not always easy, but when it comes to serious matters of security, Bonn will probably side with NATO.

The Bonn government and the German central bank have made it clear that they will insist that the economic and political unification of the Community go hand in hand. This is not simply a matter of doctrine, but in the German view a prudent insurance against the risk of foreign and economic policy adventures by other members. Certainly Washington needs to consider, however speculatively, what might be the Bonn position if, as the Germans suspect, the British and the French intend in the long run to pay no more than lip service to the idea of political union. If so, might Germany lose its enthusiasm for European economic union, and public opinion shift to an unwillingness to pay the price for abandoning the deutsche mark and an independent central bank? Germany could see itself as being offered a choice similar to that faced by a man unsure of whether to invest in individual shares or in a mutual fund.

If that happened, Germany could fall back on playing the East against the West, something its fellow Europeans wish to forestall. They fear that Germany could gain some kind of intermediate position between East and West. Chancellor Konrad Adenauer, too, hated this idea, according to Wilhelm Grewe, his ambassador to the United States, and shared the present European view that a neutralized Germany would be a catastrophe and lead to the same dilemma that existed before—having to choose between East and West.[6] No comparable figure in German history has taken Adenauer's position. My hunch, though, is that Germany will stay with economic union even if agreement on political union is delayed.

It is hard to predict how the enlargement of the European Community will affect its inner growth, but this change is bound to slow down progress toward building a federation. The growing pressure for the admission of Czechoslovakia, Poland, and Hungary is also bound to affect the character of the Community. Their influence, though, on NATO will become even more far-reaching. It would be ironic if NATO's life were to be prolonged not by its founding members but by its former adversaries. The latter know very well that within the Russian bureaucracies Cold War psychology and thought processes retain deep roots, that the military are deeply dissatisfied with the way they are being treated, and that certain Russian military forces remain on continuous alert.

THE U.S. POSITION

President Boris Yeltsin insists that he holds no animosity toward the United States. To him it is "our natural partner" to which he feels a special kinship. The United States has not reciprocated in such terms of intimacy, which would require as yet too severe mental readjustments and potential economic commitments. For the present it is enough that Russia is not seen as an enemy. It would be another irony if American relations with the European Community were to deteriorate and those with the Russian Commonwealth were to improve, though this is an evolution still hard to credit. The reason the Bush administration was slow in providing major foreign aid to the Yeltsin government is not only because foreign aid in times of an economic recession is highly unpopular or because of the huge American budget deficit, but because important, highly placed American officials have little confidence in the durability of the Russian leadership. Others argue, however, that it would be better to help keep Yeltsin in power—the most pro-American Russian leader yet—than wait for a successor who might be hard to deal with or might even revert to hostility.

If American-Russian relations improve, as Yeltsin envisages, one can imagine in the longer-range future the two countries cooperating to meet challenges from China or Japan. Meanwhile, thus far Yeltsin and his advisers lack an overall foreign policy concept; they even betray a certain naïveté in such matters. When not long ago, for instance, one of Yeltsin's closest advisers was asked by an American what he meant by an ''allied relationship,'' he ingenuously suggested it meant something like that between the United States and France, totally unaware that current Franco-American relations are almost as bad as those between Japan and America.

American public opinion is also going to affect the future of the American-European relationship. If NATO's value is insufficiently appreciated, if France continues to press ahead with its policy of ''Europe for the Europeans,'' if international trade negotiations (the so-called Uruguay Round) fail to find a compromise to overcome the bitter disagreement over the

French subsidies to its farmers (and they may well continue until the Community members refuse to subsidize the subsidies), all this could trigger a commingling of protectionism and isolationism in the United States. But though isolationist tendencies do indeed lurk just below the surface of the American public consciousness, I do not believe they will rise to dominate American political leadership. Americans today have learned too much about the advantages and necessities of world trade to fall into such fallacious nostalgia. It is true that people in a punitive mood are capable of forgetting their own real interests, but that should not happen if the United States pursues the right international economic policies. For from now on, when the Soviet threat no longer dictates a clear policy aim, economic rather than military policies are the key to American security and prosperity.

Over the last half-century American presidents have on the whole been well served by their official advisers in the field of foreign affairs and defense. One would like to think that the same quality of expertise exists in those departments that look after the nation's economic and financial interests. Alas, that is not the case. In a world where policies competent to cope with the stark economic facts of life will be the decisive factor for American influence and power, this lack of expertise is a serious drawback, one that future administrations will have to address intensively.

The United States is still a superpower militarily. In the Gulf War it deployed 20 percent of its forces—a good guide, perhaps, to the number of forces needed to be kept permanently on active duty in the future. Several allies, however, had to help to finance that war. Aid to Russia also required heavy burden sharing from the European allies. And the display of American industrialists flanking President Bush on his visit to Japan in early 1992, pleading with the Japanese to restrain their motor car exports, only underlined the American economic

infirmity. The lack of consensus about protecting the environment is another demonstration of the United States' weakened
status as a global leader. With the central military threat to the
United States largely gone, American administrations will not
be able any more to rely on declaring what they are against;
they will have to explain to their own people and to the world
what they are for.

CONCLUSION

It is already evident that the twenty-first century will be very
different from the twentieth. If the new ways are as yet unclear,
the search for them that we are witnessing is breathtaking.
First, the new members of the new Europe could succeed in
introducing democratic liberalism, free-market economies, and
the rule of international law. But no one takes their success
for granted as yet. The reformers could fail, particularly if aid
from the West to sustain this new order remains inadequate.
Everything, too, will be at risk if the United States and Russia
do not shoulder the heavy and shared burden of responsibility
to ensure the control and nonproliferation of nuclear weapons.
They are the greatest danger because even a few of them in
the hands of one small power can be a weapon of intimidation
and blackmail.

Second, because of the shared burden of responsibility, nuclear weapons could develop into the basis for a crucial political
link between the United States and Russia, to control what
remains the most dangerous threat to the survival of humanity.
However, mutual, and especially American, suspicions continue to be so deeply embedded that cooperation for nuclear
testing to nuclear waste management to space technology is
increasingly hard to organize. Some scientists believe the
American aim is simply to induce the collapse of Russian

nuclear programs by eradicating any potential for future Russian challenges; others suspect the Russians of wanting to switch to commercial uses to preserve their nuclear hegemony for future challenges. The United Nations, especially in this area, could be of great help; it has already demonstrated in Iraq that its actions are no longer automatically opposed by the Russians, whose vetoes crippled the organization almost from its inception.

Third, Americans generally resent the idea of being in charge of a Pax Americana. Also, the world is too big today for the United States to play the role the British did in the nineteenth century. Instead, the United States could create a new firm power relationship with the new Europe, designed to reinforce both sides but also to allow the development of a new political structure that could become the backbone essential to world stability for the next decade at least. And for the next century?

Isaiah Berlin, the eminent philosopher-historian, said of the current one: "I've lived through virtually the entire century, the worst century that Europe has ever had. In my life, more dreadful things occurred than at any other time in history. Worse, I suspect, even than the days of the Huns."[7] It is true that we have lived through a century dominated by impending disasters, struggles to avert disasters, and shocks of unchecked disasters. Not surprisingly, we are fearful of dashed hopes. But we can hope, as the themes of this book reflect, that after so many decades filled with dreadful and tragic events a more constructive, more promising era beckons at last.

NOTES

1. Dr. Helmut Kohl, Chancellor of the Federal Republic of Germany, speech to the Nordic Council, Helsinki, March 5, 1992, p. 9.

2. Michael Charlton, *The Price of Victory* (British Broadcasting Corporation, 1983), p. 173.

3. Ibid., p. 168.

4. See Henry Brandon, *Special Relationships: A Foreign Correspondent's Memoirs from Roosevelt to Reagan* (Atheneum, 1988), pp. 320–21.

5. General Sir Peter de la Billiere, KCB, KBE, DSO, MC, Middle East Adviser to UK Chief of the Defence Staff, "U.S. Tour—Lecture" [1991], p. 5.

6. Charlton, *Price of Victory*, pp. 106–07.

7. See Nathan Gardels, "Two Concepts of Nationalism: An Interview with Isaiah Berlin," *New York Review of Books*, vol. 38 (November 21, 1991), p. 22.

Index